MUSIC COPYRIGHT

MUSIC COPYRIGHT

An Essential Guide for the Digital Age

Casey Rae

ROWMAN & LITTLEFIELD
Lanham • Boulder • New York • London

Published by Rowman & Littlefield
An imprint of The Rowman & Littlefield Publishing Group, Inc.
4501 Forbes Boulevard, Suite 200, Lanham, Maryland 20706
www.rowman.com

6 Tinworth Street, London SE11 5AL, United Kingdom

Copyright © 2021 by Casey Rae

All rights reserved. No part of this book may be reproduced in any form or by any electronic or mechanical means, including information storage and retrieval systems, without written permission from the publisher, except by a reviewer who may quote passages in a review.

British Library Cataloguing in Publication Information Available

Library of Congress Cataloging-in-Publication Data

Names: Rae, Casey, author.
Title: Music copyright : an essential guide for the digital age / Casey Rae.
Description: Lanham, Maryland : Rowman & Littlefield Publishers, [2021] | Includes bibliographical references and index.
Identifiers: LCCN 2021014896 (print) | LCCN 2021014897 (ebook) | ISBN 9781538104835 (cloth) | ISBN 9781538104842 (paperback) | ISBN 9781538104859 (epub)
Subjects: LCSH: Copyright—Music—United States. | Copyright—Broadcasting rights—United States. | Music trade—Law and legislation—United States.
Classification: LCC KF3035 .R34 2021 (print) | LCC KF3035 (ebook) | DDC 346.7304/82—dc23
LC record available at https://lccn.loc.gov/2021014896
LC ebook record available at https://lccn.loc.gov/2021014897

CONTENTS

Abbreviations   x

Introduction   xi

1   Getting Familiar with Music Copyright   1
What Is Copyright, Anyway?   1
Copyright Is a Bundle   2
The Right to Say No   3
Expression, Fixation, and Originality   3
Copyright Terms and the Public Domain   4
Musical Works (aka Underlying Compositions or "Songs")   5
Sound Recordings   7
Exclusive Rights under Copyright   8
    Reproduction   9
    Distribution   9
    Adaptations/Derivative Works   10
    Public Performance   10
    Public Display   11

2   A Brief History of Music Copyright   13
A Limited Author's Monopoly   13
The Philosophy of Copyright   14

New Laws for a New Nation	15
Economic Incentive and Public Benefit	16
Incentives for Rights Holders	17
The First Copyright Laws	18
The Birth of Music Copyright	20
The First Copyright Society	20
Enter ASCAP	21

3 Digital Music and the Evolution of an Industry — 23

Format This!	24
Rise of the Machines	25
Raised on Radio	27
Blanket Benefits	28
Radio Is Dead, Long Live Radio	29
Analog Dreams and Digital Nightmares	29
Format Wars Redux	30
Dressed to Compress: The MP3 Era	31
The Dawn of Online Music	31
Fear of Peer to Peer	32
Online Music Goes Legitimate	32
You Win Some, YouTube Some	33
New Markets, New Methods	34
There Is No Pause Button	35

4 Musical Works and Copyright Exclusivities — 37

It All Starts with the Song	37
Reproduction/Distribution of Musical Works	38
The Mechanics of Mechanicals	39
Physical Media and "Controlled Compositions"	41
Mechanical Licensing and On-Demand Streaming	42
The Music Modernization Act and Mechanicals	44
The Mechanical Licensing Collective	45
Cover Songs and User Uploads	46
Public Performance of Musical Works	46
How Performances Licenses Work	47
Adaptations/Derivative Works	48
Copyright-Eligible Derivative Works	48
Derivative Works Categories	50

Public Display	51
Where Is My Money?	51
Music Publishers	52
Payment for Public Performance	52
Payment for Mechanicals	53
Payment for Synchronizations	53
Joint Works	53
Licensing Joint Works	54
Conclusion	55
5 Sound Recordings and Copyright Exclusivities	57
Performances Fixed in a Tangible Medium	57
The Reproduction/Distribution Right in Sound Recordings	58
The DIY Approach	59
What Labels Can Offer	60
Artist Services	61
Public Performance and Sound Recordings	61
How the Digital Performance Right for Sound Recordings Works	62
Sound Recordings as Derivative Works	64
Master Use Licenses (Synchronization)	64
Conclusion	64
6 Copyright Enforcement, Safe Harbors, and Fair Use	67
The P2P Shot Heard Around the World	67
The Era of Endless Litigation	68
Infringement Goes Mega	70
Rip It Good	71
Legislative Efforts to Combat Piracy	71
Definitions Matter	73
Takeaways from the SOPA Debate	74
Recent Developments in Online Copyright Enforcement	75
The Great DMCA Debate	76
The Ins and Outs of Internet Safe Harbors	76
Benefits of Safe Harbors	77
DMCA Pain Points	78
Watching the Detection	79
The "Value Gap"	80

	Who's the Fairest of Them All?	81
	Case Study: *Lenz v. Universal Music*	85
7	Copyright Registration, Metadata, and Databases	89
	Copyright Formalities	90
	The U.S. Copyright Office	91
	Copyright Office Divisions for Registration	92
	Why Register?	93
	Registering Joint Works	94
	When to Register and How Much Does It Cost?	95
	How to Register	96
	Preregistration Options	98
	The Review Process	99
	"Poor Man's Copyright" Debunked	100
	Copyright Notices	100
	Music Data and the Pursuit of Transparency	101
	What Is Music Metadata?	102
	Minimum Viable Data	104
	The Great Database Race	107
	Enter the Blockchain	108
	Music Blockchain Challenges	110
	Conclusion	111
8	Music Licensing: PROs, Publishing Administration, Synchronizations, and More	113
	PROs and Licensing Music for Public Performance	114
	ASCAP	115
	BMI	116
	SESAC	117
	GMR	117
	How the PRO System Works	118
	Choosing a PRO	118
	PRO Royalty Formulas	120
	Television Broadcasts	120
	Venues and Public Establishments	121
	Signing Up with a PRO	122
	Recent Legal Developments with ASCAP and BMI	123

SoundExchange: The Other PRO	123
How SoundExchange Works	125
Signing Up with SoundExchange	125
Mechanical Royalties, the Music Licensing Collective, and Publishing Administration	126
Harry Fox Agency	127
Signing up for the Mechanical Licensing Collective	127
Publishing Administration	128
Indie Aggregators and Standalone Publishing Administration	129
Signing with a Music Publisher	130
Licensing for Film, Television, Advertising, Video Games, Etc.	131
Synchronizations and Master Use Licenses	133
Types of Placements and Fee Ranges	134
Commercials	134
Movie Trailers	134
Motion Pictures	135
Television Shows	135
Video Games	136
A Note about Podcasts	136
Sync Agents and Music Libraries	136
Exclusive versus Nonexclusive	137
A Note on Copyright Reversion	137
Conclusion	138
9 Final Thoughts: Music Copyright and the Big Picture	139
Appendix	145
Notes	149
Index	157
About the Author	161

ABBREVIATIONS

A2IM	American Association of Independent Music
AFM	American Federation of Musicians
ASCAP	American Society of Composers, Authors and Publishers
BMI	Broadcast Music Incorporated
CASE Act	Copyright Alternative in Small Claims Enforcement Act
CRB	Copyright Royalty Board
DMCA	Digital Millennium Copyright Act
DNS	Domain Name Server
DOJ	Department of Justice
DPRA	Digital Performance Right in Sound Recordings Act
DRM	Digital Rights Management
DSP	Digital Service Provider
eCO	Electronic Copyright Office
EMI	Electrical and Musical Industries
GMR	Global Music Rights
HFA	Harry Fox Agency
ICE	Immigrations and Customs Enforcement
IFPI	International Federation of the Phonographic Industry
LOC	Library of Congress
MLC	Mechanical Licensing Collective
MMA	Music Modernization Act
MVD	Minimum Viable Data
NMPA	National Music Publishers Association
NOI	Notice of Intent
PRO	Performance Rights Organization
RIAA	Recording Industry Association of America
SACD	Société des Auteurs et Compositeurs Dramatiques
SACEM	Société des auteurs, compositeurs et éditeurs de musique
SAG-AFTRA	Screen Actors Guild–American Federation of Television and Radio Artists
SESAC	Society of European Stage Authors and Composers
SOPA	Stop Online Piracy Act
USCO	U.S. Copyright Office

INTRODUCTION

> Only one thing is impossible for God: To find any sense in any copyright law on the planet.
>
> —Mark Twain

Copyright is hard to wrap your head around. That's the conventional wisdom, anyway. But since when do artists pay attention to conventional wisdom? Finding your way in any field requires a fair amount of persistence and a lot of flexibility. The same could be said about learning an instrument or music production software. The good news is that copyright, like music theory or recording gear, is made up of concepts and processes that you learn. And once you do, you can use your knowledge to navigate a complex and ever-evolving marketplace for music.

Copyright is the umbrella term for certain limited-time, exclusive rights that set the rules and obligations around the use of expressive works. Okay, so what's an expressive work? It's any form of expression that can be "fixed" in a tangible medium. I'm getting a little ahead of myself, but with music, copyright is

- musical compositions (think notes and lyrics) and
- sound recordings (think performances captured on various media).

If you didn't get that the first time, don't worry—I'll repeat it often. Two copyrights in music—sound recording and underlying composition—are like déjà vu with a beat.

This book takes you step by step through the world of music copyright with an emphasis on the practical. However, if you're like me, you tend to remember stuff better when you have a sense of *why* things are the way they are. So I'll also explain the historic basis for copyright and consider how its elementary rationales hold up in our tech-driven, global music marketplace. By examining the philosophical, historic, and constructive aspects of copyright, you'll not only be in a better position to protect and advance your interests but perhaps also come to appreciate the glory and agonies of innovation and creativity.

I don't mean to sound pretentious. I wrote this book for regular people. Maybe creative people are a little irregular—that's a good thing. My point is that this isn't a dry legal treatise. It's designed to be accessible to working artists, music managers, educators, and anyone interested in the underpinnings of the music industry. I expect copyright lawyers may even get something out of it. By way of personal background, I am a musician, author, professor, and dad, but I am not a lawyer. Somehow I managed to learn this stuff, which means you can too. I was extremely fortunate to have had terrific guidance from some of the smartest music industry professionals around. Now I want to share what I've learned with you.

Although I never went to law school, I have testified in Congress on some fairly arcane copyright issues. And I've submitted numerous filings and briefs in legislative, judicial, and regulatory venues on behalf of music creators across a decade of disruption. I've designed and taught courses on the legal, technological, and entrepreneurial aspects of the music industry for prestigious colleges and universities. These days, I handle music licensing for a major audio entertainment company. I say this not to brag but rather to underscore how someone who started out with a guitar and an iffy head for business can become an expert on a subject most musicians would rate somewhere between a root canal and losing your drink tickets. And that's why I know that copyright is something you can learn. Plus it makes for great party conversation. (Well, maybe not the last part.)

INTRODUCTION

Back in the day, I had only the vaguest idea about how copyright works. On a basic level, I knew that when someone created something—a piece of music, a book, a motion picture—there were certain rights involved. I had less of a sense of what those rights were and with whom they resided. Naturally, I'd heard my share of horror stories about artists stuck in bad deals crafted by sharks in suits. I also encountered axioms like "never give up your publishing" or "pay attention to your splits." But lacking context for such wisdom, I plodded along without any sense of how copyright helps establish and sustain music careers. Many artists, including yesterday me, cling to a myth that the "business stuff" is for other people to handle. You see why there are horror stories.

There's no doubt that today's music ecosystem is more complex than that of previous decades. It's easy to feel paralyzed by a plethora of digital services and business models, to say nothing of the corresponding revenue streams—all of which are established by copyright. The antidote to this confusion is understanding, which this book aims to provide. In today's highly competitive marketplace, it's smart to have defined goals. An understanding of the bigger picture is rarer but equally useful. For music entrepreneurs, understanding how copyright works is a clear advantage. It also makes good sense. After all, you wouldn't open a bakery without knowing how dough rises.

A bit more personal background. During the 1990s and 2000s I was a performer, recording nerd, record store manager, and later a full-time music writer. The fact that I got paid for any of these activities amazes me to this day. Now they even let me write books! Looking back, I appreciate the perspectives gained from those early experiences. In many ways, I was lucky that my awareness of copyright coincided with enormous upheaval in the music business. First came CD burning, then file sharing. Now there's streaming, social media, and remix culture.

Back when I was a buyer for an independent record store, I saw how audio ripped from CDs impacted sales. Later, I witnessed labels and artists battling album leaks. When Napster arrived, there was the sense that the entire system for music distribution was about to go pear shaped. As broadband expanded, it brought a deluge of mashups, remixes, and memes—many of which use copyrighted works without permission or compensation. Some of these issues have more or less sorted themselves out; many remain challenges but also opportunities.

I also experienced these changes as a creator. Back when I began recording, artists typically had to go into a professional studio to realize their creative vision. I bought my first Pro Tools software in 1999, right around the time peer-to-peer websites arrived. The combination of democratized production and distribution made me realize there would soon be an influx of music from outside the traditional industry. Well, that happened. Today, many musicians—including well-known artists and producers—record on laptops, tablets, or even cell phones and upload their stuff straight to sites like Bandcamp and Soundcloud.

Even back in the day I believed (and still do) that artists benefit from having access to audiences. The Internet is a powerful tool for this reason. The old industry gatekeepers had their uses (and still do), but by the turn of the millennium it was getting harder and harder to break through due to corporate consolidation in the label, publishing, and broadcast sectors. As online culture began to emerge, I started asking questions. I might as well have asked my Magic 8-Ball.

- How will the economics of music work in a postscarcity world? Reply hazy; ask again later.
- Who would be the winners and losers in this transition? Cannot predict now.
- Will creators have a say in this brave new world? Don't count on it.
- What is the value of copyright in a world of infinite replicability? Better not tell you now.

We now have some answers to these questions, but several remain elusive. One thing is clear: with the Internet, access to music is no longer limited by things like shelf space or whether the DJ plays your favorite song. Distribution isn't just filling trucks with circular plastic objects for delivery to brick-and-mortar retailers. The digital transition has affected various people in various ways. I've spent a lot of time considering the impact on artists and songwriters—after all, I'm both. I've also been on the inside of major media and technology companies. Over the years, I've come to recognize that there's no single solution to all of the issues in music. But one place we might make some adjustments is copyright law. This isn't just for the sake of labels or tech companies. It's not even just for the sake of creators. Copyright is also meant to

INTRODUCTION

benefit the public. This means we have to consider the perspectives of fans, many of whom are also creators and innovators. No matter what community you're from, it is useful, even essential, to develop an understanding of how copyright functions in theory and practice. If that's your quest, you've come to the right place.

I moved to Washington, DC, in the mid-2000s because I wanted to get involved in these issues at the federal level. What a crazy idea. My obsession was figuring out how to make copyright work better alongside technological innovation, which showed no signs of letting up. I was lucky to end up working for an artist-led organization called the Future of Music Coalition, which introduced me to an impressive array of minds in the music, legal, technology, and federal policy space. I saw a lot of passionate debate. There's an inherent tension among copyright creators, copyright owners, and copyright users. I've experienced those tensions up close and (occasionally) personal. I'm glad for that because it's a reminder of why copyright is so important.

WHAT'S IN THIS BOOK

First, I'll get you up to speed on copyright as it pertains to music. I'll describe the exclusive rights that attach to expressive works and how those rights correspond to different roles and revenue flows within the music marketplace. Then I'll survey the history of copyright and provide salacious accounts of industry response to technological innovation. Fine, maybe not so salacious. Later, I'll explain how to protect and register your copyrights and update you on developments in the courts and Congress that impact how music copyright works at a granular level. And speaking of granular, I'll also describe key aspects of music licensing, including signing up for royalty collection societies, distribution, and licensing to various media.

The book is organized according to the two distinct copyrights in music: musical works and sound recordings. The exclusive rights that attach to copyright-eligible works are explained for both "sides" of the musical copyright, which lets us zero in on how music is created, distributed, and performed, along with who gets paid and how. Throughout, I've provided examples of how copyright functions in various parts of the marketplace so that you can learn from real-world examples.

Given the complexity of music copyright, it is recommended that you consult an experienced attorney on matters relevant to your rights and livelihood. That said, this book strives to present a comprehensive overview of music copyright that will hopefully serve your goals. My great wish is that you learn from the material in this book and put that knowledge to use to do amazing things in your own life and career. I'd like to thank some of the people who made a big impact on mine: Ann Chaitovitz, Kristin Thomson, Walter McDonough, Michael Bracy, Brian Zisk, Jim Griffin, Lisa Alter, George White, Bertis Downs, Dina LaPolt, Pamela Samuelson, Eddie Schwartz, Jessica Litman, Mitch Glazier, Gigi Sohn, David Israelite, Christopher Bavitz, the Honorable Mary Bono, John Simson, Charlie Sanders, Rick Carnes, David Basskin, and the late Jay Rosenthal and Sandy Pearlman.

1

GETTING FAMILIAR WITH MUSIC COPYRIGHT

WHAT IS COPYRIGHT, ANYWAY?

Most musicians and songwriters have a sense that copyright is important, but few understand why. Understanding the basics of copyright will enable you to make informed decisions, protect your expression, and hopefully earn money from others' enjoyment of your work. Before we dive into the specific aspects of how music copyright functions in the everyday world of creativity and commerce, it's important to zero in on what copyright is and, equally importantly, what it is not.

In essence, copyright is a form of property, though unlike real property—such as guitars, laptops, cars, and houses—it is "intangible," meaning that it isn't something you can grasp in your hands. Let's say you purchased a limited edition vinyl LP by your favorite band as part of Record Store Day. As the owner of a physical item containing music, you only have rights to the container, not the recordings and compositions within. The music itself belongs to its respective authors and copyright owners (these are often different entities). However, if you were to compose and record a piece of music and put it on a blank CD or flash drive that you bought from an office supply store, you own both the media storage unit *and* the music contained therein. Good for you!

COPYRIGHT IS A BUNDLE

Copyright can seem confusing because it's not one thing but rather a bundle of exclusive rights. I'll explain what these rights are, and later I'll go into more detail on how each of them functions within the music business. First, it's important to understand that these exclusive rights belong to authors the moment an expressive work is "fixed in a tangible medium."[1] Let's say there's an original melody playing in your head. That melody isn't copyrightable until it's expressed in a form that is perceivable to others. With recorded music, this includes:

- a recorded musical performance
- notes on paper or notes "embodied" in a recorded performance
- lyrics that have been written down or embodied in a recorded performance

The distinct rights within copyright confer specific, exclusive control over how such works are used, and those rights always start off with the author (or authors) of the work. However, copyrights don't always remain with their original creators. An author—and this includes songwriters and recording artists—may choose to transfer their rights to a third party, such as a label or publisher, in exchange for monetary advances and assistance in the manufacturing, distribution, and promotion of their work.

Regardless of whether an author chooses to retain their rights or assign them to another entity, the so-called exclusivities of copyright provide the mechanism for earning revenue and protecting works from being used without permission. Making money from copyright is known as "exploitation." That word has a negative connotation in other contexts, but here it simply means that works under copyright are eligible to earn revenue for their owners, authors, heirs, or estates. (A handy rule of thumb: Exploiting human beings is bad. Exploiting copyrights is good.)

THE RIGHT TO SAY NO

One important right under copyright is the ability to say no. If you create a copyrightable work and retain ownership of that work, you're under no obligation to publish it. Nor can someone else publish it against your will. Copyright also establishes legal remedies when works are used without permission. This is referred to as "infringement," also known as "piracy." (In my opinion, infringement is the more accurate term, as it covers more scenarios, including failure to pay contractually stipulated or government-set fees.) In some cases, direct permission from a copyright owner is not required, as legal and business structures have emerged for the licensing of works within a compulsory or "blanket" framework.

We'll examine various licensing scenarios soon, but for now, it's enough to know that the exclusive rights within copyright are key to preventing the unauthorized reproduction and distribution of works under copyright. It makes no difference whether the infringement generates revenue—it is a violation of law to reproduce and distribute a copyrighted work without permission from the owner or owners of that work. Period and full stop. Sometimes an artist may choose to distribute their work for free, which is their right so long as they retain ownership of the copyrighted material. However, it is important to recognize that it is copyright itself that gives creators this choice in the first place.

EXPRESSION, FIXATION, AND ORIGINALITY

Copyright is just one part of the broader universe of intellectual property that also includes patents, trademarks, and trade secrets. Unlike the other kinds of intellectual property—or IP, as they are often referred to—copyright is limited to original works of authorship: specifically, expression that is captured on paper, video audio tape, CD, hard drive, or within computer code.[2]

It is important to remember that copyright does not protect facts or ideas but rather the *expression* of facts or ideas, which is to say their unique arrangement in a fixed form. With music, fixation occurs when a song is written down or recorded. In some instances, a performance may be transmitted in real time; in such cases, the transmission is the fixation. For example, if you perform a song live on the Internet, you are fixing that song in a way that is simultaneous with its dissemination.

To be eligible for copyright, a work must be original. Congress establishes copyright protection for "original works of authorship" but has chosen not to define specifically what constitutes originality in expressive works. This may seem odd, but it was probably a good idea. If Congress had decided to lay out the specific contours of originality, it may have limited the types of works to which copyright applies. As technology progresses, it makes possible more kinds of expression. Sound recordings, for example, are a category of copyrightable works that arose from the introduction of recording devices in the late 1800s. The originality requirement essentially means that, in order to be eligible for copyright, a work can't have been copied from an existing work. This doesn't mean that the work has to be novel to qualify. For example, there are quite a few books on copyright. This one contains many salient facts that are available in other works covering the same topic. And yet, I presume to satisfy the originality requirement by virtue of how these facts are organized and expressed.

COPYRIGHT TERMS AND THE PUBLIC DOMAIN

In the United States and most of the rest of the world, expressive works remain under copyright for the lifetime of the author plus seventy additional years. For anonymous works or works made for hire (corporate authorship), the term is ninety-five years from the year of first publication or 120 years from the date of its creation, whichever ends first. Copyright terms have been a matter of intense debate in recent years. Opinions aside, the reality is that the Constitution of the United States empowers Congress to make laws around intellectual property. This includes setting the specific duration that works are protected by copyright. Congress also determines who qualifies as an author, which they have chosen to broadly define.

In the eyes of the law, authorship refers to the creator of any expressive work, including compositions, lyrics, and recordings. As previously established, copyright gives authors and rights holders control over their works for a specific duration, after which those works enter into the public domain, where they can be freely used by anyone—no permission or fee required. Because books and sheet music have been around a lot longer than recordings, there are considerably more textual works in the public domain than recordings. Eventually, however, all copyrighted material will belong to the public. Until then, the owners of the various kinds of expressive works enjoy exclusive rights over how those works are used.

To fully grasp how music copyright works in practice, we must have a sense of the specific rights conferred to authors and owners of copyright. But first, I'll remind you once again that there are *two distinct copyrights in music*: the musical work and the sound recording. Understanding both sides is essential to decoding how the music industry functions. It will also save you a lot of headaches when it comes to protecting your interests and positioning your music in the marketplace. Most, but not all, of these exclusive rights apply to both musical works and sound recordings. Understanding which rights apply and under what conditions is the key that unlocks the entirety of music copyright. Let's dive in.

MUSICAL WORKS (AKA UNDERLYING COMPOSITIONS OR "SONGS")

You can think of musical works as lyrics or notes on paper; sometimes they are referred to as "compositions" or "underlying compositions," or more simply "songs." Musical works enjoy a separate and distinct copyright apart from the sound recordings in which they are embodied. Consider this: There is no such thing as a musical sound recording that does not contain an underlying composition. If you write the music for a song, or its lyrics, you are the exclusive rights holder of that musical work. If you collaborate with another songwriter, you control the portion of the musical work for which you are the author (this is sometimes referred to as your "split"). In the world of songwriting, it's not unusual

Figure 1.1. Early American sheet music.
Source: **U.S. Library of Congress.**

for there to be multiple contributors to a musical work, which is why music publishing—the term of art for the exploitation of compositions—is one of the more complicated (and often contentious) areas of the music business.

You don't need to write down the actual musical notes as long as the composition is embodied in a "tangible medium"—for example, audio tape or computer hard drive. Sheet music is an example of a composition being fixed in a tangible medium, but these days, it's more common for songwriters to "fix" compositions in demo recordings to serve as reference for later performer(s) (figure 1.1).

Lyrics are considered part of the musical work, though they may be authored by different parties than those who composed the music—in which case, the lyrical portion belongs to the lyricist and the composition to whomever wrote the music. Composers or lyricists can choose to transfer their respective portions of the song to a publisher who will exploit these splits under specific contractual provisions. It is not uncommon for a contemporary pop song to have a dozen writers and perhaps as many publishers, which can make licensing musical works a challenge. I'll get into all of that in upcoming chapters on copyright registration, metadata, databases, and music licensing.

SOUND RECORDINGS

The other "side" of music copyright is sound recordings, which are sometimes referred to as "master recordings," or simply "masters." (You probably have heard about artists attempting to "get their masters back" from a label, which can pose legal hurdles.) It's easiest to think of sound recordings as performances captured on tape, CD, or hard drive. Control of a sound recording resides with the performer until such time that ownership is transferred to a third party, such as a label. (Labels often sign artists *before* recordings are made, under provisions that automatically transfer ownership of recordings made while the artist is under contract.) If the performing artist chooses not to transfer their sound recordings, as is increasingly common these days, they will enjoy exclusive rights over the recordings for the life of the copyright.

In some ways, sound recordings are more straightforward than musical works in terms of authorship. A single featured performer may be considered the author if the backing musicians' contributions are work for hire (though they may still be eligible for certain royalties, such as those from digital public performance). If the recording is made by a band, the members of the band will decide how to split revenue from its exploitation. In some instances, a producer may have a claim to authorship based on their contributions to creating the sound recording.

As previously mentioned, signing with a label requires a transfer of sound copyrights, including those yet to be made during the contractual term. However, under the 1976 Copyright Act, all authors—including recording artists—are eligible after thirty-five years to file notice with the copyright owner and the U.S. Copyright Office to reclaim previously transferred rights. This is called "termination of transfer," which I describe in greater detail in chapter 8. For now, just keep in mind that some labels have taken the view that artists aren't eligible to recapture their sound recordings. This seems contrary to the intent of Congress to give *all* authors a second bite at the apple with regard to their creative expression.

Believe it or not, sound recordings did not enjoy federal copyright protection until February 15, 1972. Before that, they were a matter of state law, and that tended to be only in places where there was an established industry for the manufacturing and distribution of recorded music. In advance of the last complete update of the Copyright Act in 1976 (which went into effect in 1978), labels successfully lobbied to have sound recordings recognized by the federal government as a distinct copyright apart from musical works. However, only sound recordings made after February 15, 1972, qualify for full federal protections. That leaves a great many recordings made by so-called legacy artists in a legal gray area. I'll describe how this impacts certain uses of sound recordings in chapter 5.

Now that we have a better understanding of the two-sided coin that is music copyright, it's time to familiarize ourselves with the individual, exclusive rights conferred upon authors and owners of copyright. These rights apply to a variety of expressive works, including books, articles, photographs, dramatic works, motion pictures, choreography, pantomime, and computer code. Our focus here will be what these exclusivities mean for songwriters, recording artists, and rights holders.

EXCLUSIVE RIGHTS UNDER COPYRIGHT

Now we know that copyright is "born" when an author "fixes" their expression in a tangible medium, regardless of whether that work is officially registered with the U.S. Copyright Office. (Registration is important for other reasons, including the ability to seek damages for infringement; chapter 7 examines the benefits of registration and the process for doing so.)

Copyright gives authors—including musicians and composers—the means for deriving revenue from their work, as well as the ability to prevent others from using their work in ways to which the author objects. Exploitation and enforcement of copyright depends on the rights established by the U.S. Constitution and further enumerated by Congress. Let's now look at what these rights encompass, with the understanding that we'll be spending a lot more time with each of them as we explore how music copyright works in practice.

Reproduction

This is the right to reproduce a work. In music, the reproduction right concerns compositions, lyrics, and sound recordings. For example, if you record your own performance of a song that you wrote, you have exclusive rights to make copies of both the composition and the recording. That is, until you decide to assign that right to a third party, such as a label or publisher, in exchange for an advance, marketing and distribution support, and the payment of royalties under contractual provision. Once an expressive work is fixed in a tangible medium, the right to make reproductions—the "copy" in copyright—belongs exclusively to the author until such a time that a transfer of copyright is made.

Distribution

This is the right to distribute the work to the public by sale, rental, lease, or lending. Similar to the right of reproduction, the distribution right gives authors of expressive works the exclusive right to disseminate their works to the public. With musical works, this applies only to the initial distribution. After that, the right falls under a compulsory licensing framework with a government-set rate. For example, if you write a song, you alone enjoy the right to make it available for the first time. After that, anyone is free to make a recording embodying your underlying composition, so long as they pay the compulsory license fee (currently 9.1 cents for recordings up to five minutes and 1.75 cents per minute for tracks over five minutes). This compulsory license, which we will examine more closely in chapter 2, allows artists to record cover songs without having to ask permission, so long as the copyrightable elements of the original composition are not significantly altered. It also lets labels release recordings embodying musical works provided they pay the compulsory license fee. Authors of both musical works and sound recordings are free to assign their rights to third parties, such as publishers and record labels.

Adaptations/Derivative Works

This is the right to alter or modify a work or to create a new work in another medium based on or using elements of the original. (In music, remixes and mashups are considered derivative works; this is another area of intense industry debate.) Making significant changes to lyrics would also be an example of derivative activity that requires permission from the copyright owner. Whether a new work based on a previous work is sufficiently transformative to enjoy a separate copyright from the original depends on several factors. However, permission from the author or owner of the original work is always required and usually involves a fee. (The fair use doctrine in copyright law allows for the use of portions of existing works under specific conditions; this will be further discussed in chapter 6.)

Public Performance

This refers to the exclusive right to "perform" the music in public. Things can get a bit tricky here, as compositions and sound recordings are treated differently depending on where the performance occurs. For example, in the United States, sound recordings have a limited performance right that applies only to noninteractive digital transmission (satellite and cable radio, as well as webcasts) but not over-the-air, AM/FM broadcasts. Unlike musical works, there is no public performance right for sound recordings played in bars, nightclubs, restaurants, hotel lobbies, or any other public venue. The performance right for musical works, on the other hand, extends to the use of compositions in all public venues (whether the music is live or prerecorded), as well as noninteractive digital *and* analog transmission (AM/FM radio, digital radio, and television broadcasts). If this seems confusing, don't worry—I'll further demystify the performance right in chapters 4 and 5.

Public Display

This is the right to display a copyrighted work publicly. For music, this concerns only compositions (notes and lyrics), not sound recordings. For example, lyrics depicted in a photograph as part of a public exhibit would qualify, as would the same lyrics on screen in a motion picture or television show. This right also extends to motion picture and television stills featuring musical works, along with various types of slides. Public display is less common in the music industry, but it does occur, and it is part of the exclusive rights conferred to authors and owners of copyright.

Now that you have a basic understanding of the specific rights that attach to expressive works, I'll unpack the rationale behind copyright and how it has evolved over the history of the music industry. This will give you a sense of how existing law came to be and may inspire some ideas about how copyright might evolve to meet current and emerging challenges. Go ahead, turn the page.

2

A BRIEF HISTORY OF MUSIC COPYRIGHT

Now we understand some basic things about copyright. We know that it is a type of intellectual property, which is an intangible subset of personal property. We understand that it is a bundle of exclusive rights that originate with authors of expressive works. And we are aware that to qualify for copyright, works must be original and fixed in a tangible form. We recognize that copyright doesn't cover ideas themselves but rather their expression. And we've learned that, unlike other kinds of property, copyright comes with an expiration date. All of this is by design—the authors of the first copyright laws could have easily adopted the rules governing physical property, which are considered an extension of an individual person—a so-called "natural right."[1] Instead, they chose to set limits on the so-called author's monopoly. I'll tell you why that is, along with a brief history of how technology—from the earliest recordings on wax cylinders to the Internet—has shaped how music copyright has evolved over the decades.

A LIMITED AUTHOR'S MONOPOLY

Some might prefer copyright to be absolute property belonging to authors and rights holders for eternity. But this is not the case. Copyright protections exist only for a set period of time before works permanently enter the public domain, at which point anyone is free to exploit, transform, or incorporate aspects of previously copyrighted material. True, the length of time that works exist under copyright has been considerably extended since the original term of fourteen years under the 1790 Copyright Act. Likewise, the law has, over the decades, been updated to include more kinds of works and uses of works. Such expansions of copyright were in many instances designed to accommodate new technologies that in turn have aided the creation and dissemination of works. Many would argue that current copyright law needs to be updated in order to meet the realities of the digital age. I agree and believe that history can show us how reform might be achieved. Let's take a quick look back at how copyright came to be so we can get a sense of where it might be going.

THE PHILOSOPHY OF COPYRIGHT

Just as music itself is governed by rules of theory—tones, intervals, harmonic relationships, meter, etc.—copyright is rooted in essential principles about how expression should be treated as a matter of property. Because copyright (and intellectual property in general) differs from physical items that we can possess, it rests on certain assumptions that arose from earlier debates about the nature of ideas.

One thing to keep in mind as you read the next sections: I'll be focusing on American copyright law and its underlying philosophies. Other countries have different emphases when it comes to balancing the interests of authors and the public. Nevertheless, most nations with developed culture industries share a common outlook with regard to the right of authors to derive benefit from their creative labors. This shared understanding has inspired efforts to harmonize international intellectual property law to some degree of success. Many challenges remain, however, especially as technology enables more people in more places to become authors and distributors of copyright.

NEW LAWS FOR A NEW NATION

At the dawn of the American experiment, Thomas Jefferson, Founding Father and chief author of the Declaration of Independence, expressed many opinions about what form copyright should take. He viewed ideas and their expression as gifts to humanity and saw the benefit in these gifts being widely spread. Jefferson recognized the enrichment that can come from being exposed to the ideas of others and believed that America's intellectual property laws should reflect this value. He also believed that the *expression* of ideas—the fruit of intellectual activity—was distinct from other forms of property:

> He who receives an idea from me, receives instruction himself without lessening mine; as he who lights his taper at mine, receives light without darkening me. That ideas should freely spread from one to another over the globe, for the moral and mutual instruction of man, and improvement of his condition, seems to have been peculiarly and benevolently designed by nature, when she made them, like fire, expansible over all space, without lessening their density in any point, and like the air in which we breathe, move, and have our physical being, incapable of confinement or exclusive appropriation.[2]

Copyright was therefore devised to benefit two parties: authors and the public. Of course, authors are also members of the public—like anyone else, they benefit from access to edifying, entertaining, challenging, and inspiring works. However, it often takes sweat, time, and monetary investment to bring a work forward, which is why copyright confers exclusive, limited-time rights to authors. It is through these rights that creators derive revenue, which has long been considered a crucial incentive to production. That being said, there are instances when copyright can limit access, which is why protections only last for a set duration, after which anyone is free to make use of the work in any manner they see fit. Article 1, Section 8, Clause 8 of the United States Constitution lays out the balance the Framers intended for America's intellectual property regime. It empowers Congress to promote the progress of science and useful arts, by securing for limited times to authors and inventors the exclusive right to their respective writings and discoveries.

And there you have it—a not entirely inelegant compact for the ages. What could go wrong? Plenty, as it turns out. But a lot of important things go right.

ECONOMIC INCENTIVE AND PUBLIC BENEFIT

The overarching goal of copyright is to incentivize the creation of new works and promote their availability to the public. The interests in copyright aren't always in perfect alignment, however. Sometimes the author's benefit runs contrary to that of the public or vice-versa. Nevertheless, it is a system that has served its purpose well for more than two hundred years. Consider your favorite songs, books, movies, TV shows, and the like—chances are, you may never have come across those works absent the economic incentive provided by copyright. Of course, the argument has been made that creative people will produce works whether or not they get paid. And that's probably true. Nevertheless, the ability to derive revenue from expressive works helps artists pay the bills, which enables them to keep on creating (and for the public to keep on enjoying their creativity).

Like anyone in a free society, authors of expressive works have the right to be compensated for their labors, provided there is sufficient demand. Copyright strikes a balance between the interests of creators and that of the public by establishing incentives for the broad distribution of copyrighted works. This includes the companies that invest in the creation and dissemination of works. There are a number of benefits to the public:

- more works are available due to the economic incentive to create them
- access to expressive works inspires other authors to create expressive works of their own
- all copyrighted works will eventually be free for anyone to use, modify, and build upon

INCENTIVES FOR RIGHTS HOLDERS

Not all parties with an economic interest in copyright are authors. There are various companies whose primary function is to bring expressive works to the market. Most of these companies seek monetary reward for doing so. Although record labels and music publishers are sometimes criticized for foisting onerous contracts on artists, they also invest in music that we know and love. It's true that the Internet has leveled the playing field in terms of access to audiences, but making audiences aware of artists can be an expensive proposition. While there are examples of music and other media "going viral" without a concerted marketing push, the reality is that, with fewer gatekeepers, there is ever more competition. Such is life in the attention economy.

Labels, for example, invest in artists whose music they believe will find traction with fans, though this is hardly a guarantee even with millions of dollars spent on marketing. It's no wonder, then, that music companies are highly attuned to the return on their investments. And that means seeking the best possible deals where direct negotiation is permitted by law (and where it isn't, lobbying the government for increased rates under compulsory frameworks). It also involves copyright enforcement, which is a vortex of fear and loathing.

Given the complexities of copyright and the rapid pace of technological development, some have suggested blowing up the whole system and starting over. That would be difficult to do given that copyright is part of the U.S. Constitution. I understand why some people are skeptical of the major labels and publishers. But getting rid of copyright would impact individual creators as much, perhaps more, than it would harm big corporations. Remember, not all music companies are giant multinationals. Some are mom-and-pop outfits who are as passionate about music as you are. It's not just about the superstars either. These days, we see more and more artists and songwriters who are completely independent. Without copyright, what guarantees would they have regarding compensation and respect for their work?

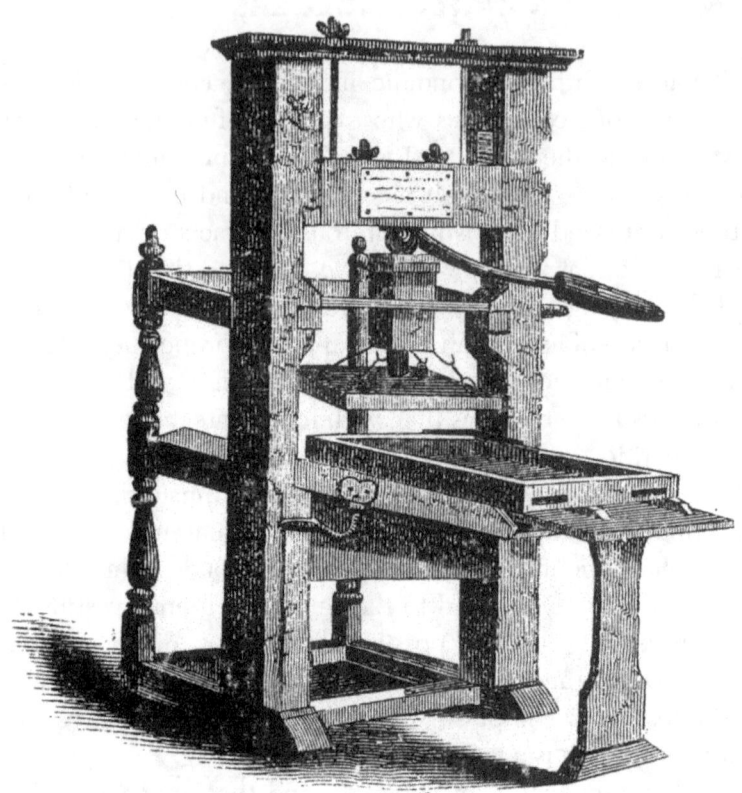

Figure 2.1. Early printing press.

THE FIRST COPYRIGHT LAWS

Originally, copyright applied only to printed material like maps and books, but over the years, protections have extended to all kinds of works of authorship, including music. The arrival of the printing press in the fifteenth century created a new opportunity for the broader dissemination of information, which in turn established the conditions for the first laws around intellectual property in Europe (figure 2.1). Before movable type, reproducing texts was a laborious, time-consuming affair chiefly undertaken by government officials or scholarly priests. Once mechanical printing became common, many different kinds of books, tracts, and pamphlets became available to the public. This didn't always sit well with the powers that be. Actually, monarchs and religious officials of the time sought to control information they deemed critical to the ruling class by requiring book publishers—or stationers, as they were known in England—to operate under the king's seal. The Licensing Act of 1622 was Great Britain's earliest attempt at establishing a legal framework for works of authorship. It established a register of printed material overseen by a group called the Stationers' Company, which was obligated to comply with royal censorship. When that law expired, a new one was passed that for the first time recognized the rights of authors. And thus, copyright was born.

The Statute of Anne, adopted by England in 1710, is considered the world's first copyright law. This law limited the monopoly that publishers previously enjoyed over printed material, establishing a copyright term of fourteen years, after which works would enter the public domain. The act vested initial ownership with the author of a work, which helped establish the publishing industry by creating the conditions through which authors could transfer their rights to a third party in exchange for up-front revenue or royalties from sales. This is the same formula under which the copyright industries—including the music business—continue to operate. Nowadays, self-publishing is a more realistic option due to the advent of the Internet—a technology easily as disruptive as the printing press. Nevertheless, the transfer of copyright from author to publisher is still very common—this book is but one example. Reasons for transferring one's copyright include:

- monetary advances that enable authors to produce works
- technical assistance in creating works
- reproduction and distribution of works
- promotion of works to the public
- negotiating fees for uses of works

Depending on circumstances, this might make sense for a pop star or a pamphleteer. But let's linger a bit longer in the eighteenth century. So influential was the Statute of Anne that the United States essentially plagiarized it when establishing its first laws around intellectual property. The requirement for Congress to do so was put forth in the fundamental framework for American governance, the U.S. Constitution, ratified in 1788. The Constitution's so-called commerce clause provides for the entirety of America's intellectual property laws. Without it, Congress could not have extended copyright to include forms of expression beyond printed texts, maps, and charts (the only stuff named in the Copyright Act of 1790). Because the legislative branch makes the actual rules, it wasn't long before composers and publishers began lobbying Congress to include music. And that's where things get interesting.

THE BIRTH OF MUSIC COPYRIGHT

As I mentioned, the first copyright laws applied only to published text, maps, and charts. Next came sheet music, which gave authors and publishers of such works control over the reproduction and distribution of musical notation and lyrics on paper. However, if someone were to perform those notes and lyrics in public, composers and publishers had no way to be paid. Nor could they prevent such performances from happening. And so they began pushing for laws to cover the public performance of their works. This was an early example of how copyrights might be exploited beyond reproduction and distribution. As a matter of efficiency, it was necessary to establish systems for the collective management of copyrights. And that's how performance rights organizations (PROs) first came to be.

THE FIRST COPYRIGHT SOCIETY

France was ahead of the game when it came to public performance rights. In 1777, the Bureau de Legislation Dramatique was established to collect fees on behalf of playwrights and comedians. By 1829, the organization had become the Société des Auteurs et Compositeurs Dramatiques (SACD), which still exists today to manage theatrical, audiovisual, and photographic works. Music became part of the performance rights bundle in 1847, when lyricist Ernest Bourget had a spat with the owners of the Café des Ambassadeurs. An artists' rights movement was born when Bourget refused to pay for drinks because he had not received a single franc for the performances of his works at the venue. The dispute eventually went to trial, leading to the formation of the world's first musical PRO, the Société des auteurs, compositeurs et éditeurs de musique, commonly referred to as SACEM. To this day, the rights of French songwriters, composers, and publishers are collectively managed by SACEM.

ENTER ASCAP

In 1897, the publishers of musical works in the United States successfully lobbied Congress to establish America's first performance right for music. With this new legal protection, composers and publishers were enabled to collect money whenever someone publicly performed their compositions. As was the case in France, the new law meant that any American venue that offered musical entertainment was required to pay a fee. However, it wasn't easy to collect this money, and the owners of the establishments were by no means eager to pay. And so in 1917 America's first performing rights organization was formed. The American Society of Composers, Authors and Publishers (ASCAP) established itself by making sure that anyone publicly performing music honored their obligation under law to pay composers and publishers. That mission continues to this day, with a handful of other PROs following suit.

In subsequent decades, additional legislation was enacted to protect the interests of creators and owners of music copyright. These laws served as the cornerstone of America's music industry. Technology also played a major role in the evolution of copyright law. It expanded the ways in which people access expressive works and how those works can be used, which required statutory updates, including the establishment of new rights and exceptions. Much as the printing press revolutionized how text-based material was produced and distributed, advances in technology made it possible for music to reach more people than ever before and for new forms of creativity and business models to emerge as part of this evolution.

In the next chapter, I'll describe how technology has impacted copyright and the music industry over the past few decades—from major rights holders, to individual creators and music entrepreneurs, to digital innovators. Then I'll dive back into exclusivities, this time broken out by musical works and sound recordings—the twin pillars of the music copyright multiverse.

3

DIGITAL MUSIC AND THE EVOLUTION OF AN INDUSTRY

Copyright has evolved in response to technological innovation, often struggling to keep up with the pace of change. It's been this way across the decades, from phonographic records to radio to downloads to the Internet. Because much of the music industry operates within copyright law, its prime movers have been very involved in these developments. Responses to technology among corporate music leaders has been more or less predictable. The default position is most often resistance, then, eventually, accommodations are reached that almost always end up enriching those same executives. Occasionally, Congress gets involved.

But not very often. Passing legislation can be a slow and contentious process with no guaranteed outcome. To wit: The last time the Copyright Act got a top-to-bottom overhaul was way back in 1976, with preliminary discussions kicking off in the 1950s. The prior revamp was in 1909. These days, twenty years is like two centuries in tech time. (If it's major, hit me on my pager!) The challenge is devising laws that won't be obsolete as soon as the ink dries. That's not to say it isn't worth the effort. Entire business sectors and cultural communities have been born from the often tense interplay between copyright and technology. It's a dense history, so I'll only offer highlights, starting with the now centuries-old battle over music formats.

FORMAT THIS!

The battle over music formats begins with a legend of American ingenuity, Thomas Edison, whose groundbreaking wax cylinder was afforded a patent in 1877 (figure 3.1). Edison's "records" contained small surface etches, converted into audible sound with the aid of a specially designed mechanical phonograph. A technological marvel plagued by poor fidelity, cylinders degraded each time they were played, limiting their value beyond novelty. Nevertheless, they were successfully marketed and sold to the public, some of who became the first record collectors. A nascent recording industry soon emerged, with Columbia Phonograph and Blue Amberol slapping their brand names on cylinders containing ditties like "Auld Lang Syne" and "Whistle and I'll Wait for You." And that's why recorded music companies are to this day called labels.

Edison's cylinders were game changers. No longer was it necessary to attend a revue or purchase sheet music to enjoy the tunes of the day. Demand for records increased, driving manufacturers to experiment with ways to improve sound quality. A major advancement came with

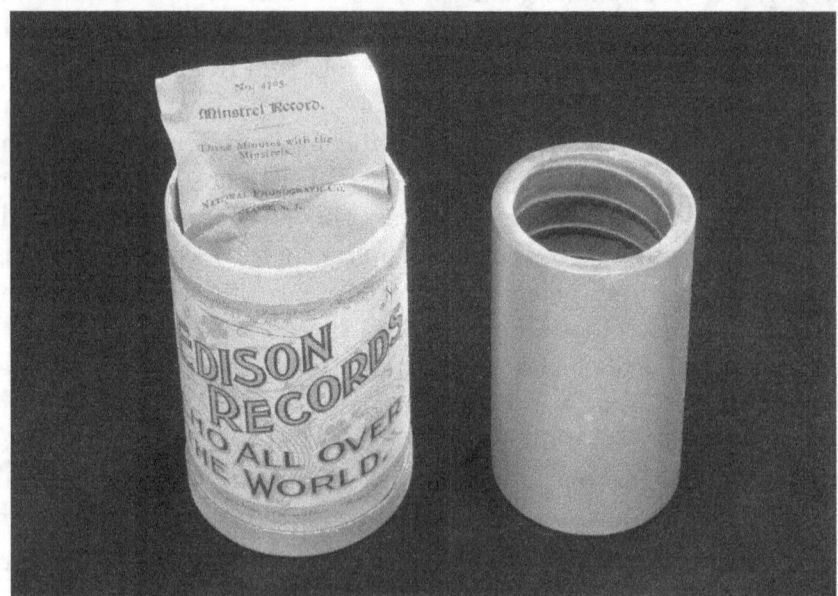

Figure 3.1. Edison wax cylinder. *Source:* USCB Cylinder Audio Archive.

the arrival of the flat phonographic disc, invented by Emil Berliner in part to avoid paying a licensing fee to Edison. Berliner's gramophone appeared in the late 1800s and made use of a special stylus that traced the surface of a flat, round surface familiar to vinyl fetishists (no, the other kind). This innovation greatly improved sound quality, was a simpler device for playback, and could be more easily mass produced. Victrola introduced its legendary gramophone in 1906, which soon became the gold standard in home audio playback. By the turn of the century, flat discs had displaced cylinders among paleo music consumers.

Labels soon became more significant, entrenching their dominance by consolidating manufacturing and distribution capabilities. The 1930 merger of the Gramophone Company and the Columbia Gramophone Company resulted in the formation of Electrical and Musical Industries (EMI), heralding a trend of mergers and acquisitions in the recorded music marketplace that continues to this day. By the 1920s and 1930s, the record business enjoyed brisk sales, with revenue continuing on an upward trajectory until the Great Depression briefly disrupted its groove. After that, the business rebounded with the arrival of the long-play vinyl format in 1948.

RISE OF THE MACHINES

Another development that directly impacted copyright was the emergence of so-called player pianos around 1900. These devices operated using paper rolls with punched-in holes that triggered a sequence of notes to be performed "mechanically" by the piano keyboard. The popularity of player pianos motivated music publishers to seek fees for the use of their compositions in these newfangled contraptions. In 1909, Congress bowed to pressure and established the first "mechanical royalty" as part of its comprehensive update of the Copyright Act. This new right required anyone who made a reproduction of a composition for the purposes of automated playback to pay a fee to music publishers (who in turn would compensate composers and lyricists based on agreement). This law didn't just apply to player pianos, however. It also meant that whenever a record label made a sound recording embodying a composition—as all musical recordings do—they were required to pay

Figure 3.2. Advertisement for an early Columbia LP.

a mechanical royalty to the publishers. (This is also true if you record a cover of an existing composition; more on that in the next chapter.)

Mechanical royalties were subsequently applied to physical media such as LPs, cassettes, and CDs because the recordings they contain are based on underlying compositions that can be played on various devices (figure 3.2). This obligation was eventually extended to online media such as downloads and on-demand streams. However, with the likes of Spotify or Apple Music, it isn't the labels who are required to pay mechanical royalties to the publishers but the services themselves. The reasoning is that, given the complexity of on-demand music (which the law calls "interactive"), the services are in a better position to track usage and pay publishers. Recent legislation moved download stores into the same category as on-demand streaming for the purposes of paying mechanical royalties.[1]

Note: Noninteractive services such as terrestrial radio, satellite radio, and webcasts (where the user is not able to choose which specific song or album they want to hear) are not required to pay a mechanical royalty. AM/FM broadcasters and digital radio do pay *performance* royalties, but they don't pay the same parties. (Chapters 4 and 5 cover performance rights for musical works and sound recordings, so you'll become more familiar with this part of music copyright and its weird exceptions.)

RAISED ON RADIO

In the late 1800s, another technology arrived that would expand the market for recorded music. Initially developed as a military communications platform, radio soon grew to include musical and other entertainments. But it wasn't until the advent of commercial radio in the 1920s that the broadcast market began to take shape. With revenue generated from advertising, programming aimed to attract and retain listeners. Music, live or on phonograph, was a big draw for early radio audiences, and it remains a big draw today.

It's hard to imagine, but music publishers once saw radio as a disruptive technology. Why? Because more people listened to the radio than could fit in the largest music halls. And if those same people heard their favorite song on the radio every day, why would they bother buying the sheet music? Like the Internet to come, copyright owners grappled with radio's popularity and scale, both of which made it hard to assert their exclusive rights under copyright law.

The lack of a licensing framework for radio frustrated publishers' attempts to derive revenue from the new technology. It drove them crazy because they knew broadcasters were making money selling ads to listeners who tuned in for the music (and *The Shadow*, obviously; that show is awesome). The record labels took a more favorable view, but unless they moonlighted in publishing, they didn't own a copyright between them (remember, labels didn't get rights in sound recordings until 1972).

Sales of recorded music declined in commercial radio's early years due to the Great Depression, which sapped consumer spending and swept labels out of business. As the economy recovered, radio's true value to the music industry became apparent: broadcasting put asses in seats and stimulated record sales. This is why, in the United States at least, labels were for years willing to overlook the fact that AM/FM radio is not required to pay performance royalties for sound recordings. And that is true to this day. However, as the industry has shifted to "plays-based" economics, labels and recording artists are pushing harder for a terrestrial radio performance right.

Note: Digital radio services *do* pay a performance royalty on both sides of the music copyright. This is explained in more detail in upcoming chapters.

BLANKET BENEFITS

Back to those wily music publishers. Having managed to persuade Congress to give them a performance right, they wasted little time seeking fees from broadcasters. Now, they may have had the right, but it was near impossible to get paid. And thus, "blanket licenses" were born. This new approach to permission and compensation allowed composers and publishers to license all of their songs in exchange for up-front fees. Stations could play any music they wanted provided they were licensed by ASCAP. Problem solved? Not exactly. Broadcasters were unhappy with ASCAP's aggressive fees and tactics and complained to the federal government. Their argument had merit: ASCAP controlled the vast majority of desirable repertoire and were in a position to abuse their market power. Which is why, in 1941, ASCAP agreed to enter a so-called consent decree issued by the U.S. Department of Justice.

Shortly before that all went down, broadcasters attempted to spark competition in the performance licensing marketplace by creating Broadcast Music Incorporated (BMI) in 1939. Then—bam!—BMI was slammed with a consent decree the same year as ASCAP. Though considered nonadmissions of guilt, the consent decrees place real conditions on PRO behavior. First, ASCAP and BMI must offer licenses on equivalent terms—no playing favorites or acts of market retribution. Second, the blanket licenses must be nonexclusive, meaning a licensor is free to license the same repertoire to other users. Third, if a user takes a license, they are allowed to perform any and all songs in the PRO's repertoire. If parties fail to agree on fees, matters are settled in what's known as rate court. These rules remain in place today.

RADIO IS DEAD, LONG LIVE RADIO

Some in music and tech call radio a "horse and buggy technology," one destined to be replaced by the Internet. I can tell you that reports of radio's demise are greatly exaggerated. Broadcasting remains a powerhouse industry, both in terms of listenership and revenue (to say nothing of lobbying influence). Radio's no-cost-to-the-listener ubiquity has served its longevity. It is estimated that 93 percent of Americans encounter broadcast radio on a weekly basis, with 243 million monthly listeners.[2] Surprisingly, millennials are among the largest audience demographic, with around 66.5 million younger listeners tuning in each week.[3] As of 2017, commercial radio is a $13.87 billion industry.[4] That last figure makes the exemption allowing broadcasters to not pay artists and labels that much more stunning. Doubly so when compared to almost every other country on the planet that does pay. Worse, U.S. artists and labels are unable to collect royalties for foreign plays due to the lack of a "reciprocal" right. If parity in copyright law is a goal, this loophole must be closed.

ANALOG DREAMS AND DIGITAL NIGHTMARES

As demand for recorded media grew in the decades following the introduction of the phonographic disc, so too did music labels' desire for a copyright in sound recordings. Concerned about piracy via home taping and bootleg vinyl presses, labels argued that federal protections were essential to protecting their interests. On February 15, 1972, Congress passed a law conferring copyright on sound recordings "fixed" after the date of enactment. Recordings made before February 15, 1972, were not retroactively granted copyright protections but were instead covered under state laws until 2067, when all of these older recordings will simultaneously enter the public domain. The establishment of a federal copyright for sound recordings increased the leverage of the record labels and gave their lobbying and legal arm, the Recording Industry Association of America—which had previously focused on product standards and sales thresholds—a whole new sandbox to play in.

Format Wars Redux

For the better part of a century, records were the playback media of choice (they also happened to be one of the only playback media). That market exploded when Columbia introduced the twelve-inch, 33 RPM disc in 1948. This new format sounded way better than the previous 78 RPM discs (sorry vintage hot jazz fans) and held way more music than 45s. Playback innovation didn't stop there: other formats include eight-track cartridges, cassettes, and the more niche reel-to-reel. The real game changer, at least in terms of industry profits, arrived in August 1982. Developed in partnership between the Sony and Philips corporations, the compact disc, or CD, employs digital encoding of audio and laser optic playback in a piece of plastic that holds more musical information than a single LP.

Unlike later DVDs, CD manufacturers opted not to use digital rights management, or DRM—a kind of "lock" that theoretically prevents copying. Personal computers with CD burning drives soon had music executives wishing they'd made a different choice. Nevertheless, CDs gave labels an opportunity to persuade fans to buy music they already owned in other formats such as vinyl, eight-track, and cassette. It worked! Entire catalogs by beloved artists were artists repurchased, and the very first digital-age stars were born. Publishers and songwriters did well too, as sales of recordings embodying their underlying compositions made it rain mechanicals.

Labels at first resisted CDs, fearing that they would cannibalize sales of other formats. Which did end up happening. But even after CDs became the dominant format, industry profits only swelled. In 1994, sales of recorded music were over $12.1 billion in the United States alone.[5] This highlights a recurring dynamic with technology and the music business. First, the new technology is feared, rejected, or attacked. It's not entirely irrational: big companies in particular want to protect their business models and usually aren't shy about asserting their rights. I'm not trying to argue a false dichotomy, and I appreciate the diversity of views on these matters. I'm merely noting how emerging technologies tend to be viewed by high-level music executives, at least at first. Later, new revenue streams emerge and the industry adapts. With CDs, it was a revenue tsunami. That is, until the MP3 came along.

Dressed to Compress: The MP3 Era

If you were a music creator, a music executive, or a music fan at the turn of the millennium, you already know what a big deal the MP3 was. When this new format hit the World Wide Web, it changed music forever. What MP3s lacked in audio fidelity they made up for in digital utility. Using a compression algorithm that allowed for the more efficient distribution of audio files over the Internet, MP3s were unencrypted by default. That meant rights holders had no control over their distribution. What they did have was lawyers.

Labels first went after portable digital music players that used the MP3 format. They weren't very successful. *Recording Industry Association of America v. Diamond Multimedia Systems, Inc.* was about whether the manufacturers of the Diamond Rio MP3 player had to pay royalties under the Audio Home Recording Act. That's not clear to this day, but it doesn't matter because that MP3 player is now as extinct as decorum in politics. At any rate, the final ruling also said that it's okay to move MP3 files from your computer to your MP3 player, an interpretation rooted in prior legal precedent.[6] That was enough for Steve Jobs to move forward with Apple's iPod, perhaps an even bigger game changer.

If labels couldn't kill the MP3 player, they could push for digital music files to have locks (the aforementioned DRM). The iPod, which hit shelves in October 2001, was able to store and play back DRM-free MP3s. But Apple's digital music storefront, iTunes—which arrived the same year and was expanded to Windows systems in 2003—had DRM on every track it sold.[7] CEO Jobs complained about DRM, but his company nevertheless benefited from it. Apple's DRM-enabled "walled garden," along with the popularity of the iPod and iTunes, resulted in the company becoming America's largest music retailer by 2008.

THE DAWN OF ONLINE MUSIC

When I think back on music and the Internet, sure I remember the fights about file sharing, but I also recall the thrill of putting your music out to the world. Or at least the Internet-connected world, which at that time was brimming with camaraderie and joie de vivre (can you imagine?). Even before MySpace, there were sites like MP3.com where musicians could post tracks that plenty of real people actually listened to. And then the lawyers came. That was probably to be expected because another thing MP3.com let users do was upload their digital music collections, including, one presumes, works under copyright. In 2000, a federal judge held MP3.com liable for infringement. Ironically, the site functioned a lot like the cloud storage services today offered by the likes of Amazon, Google, and Apple. I guess being first isn't always best. Just ask the Diamond Rio MP3 player. (If you can find one.)

Fear of Peer to Peer

Think about it: We went from a music marketplace where fans had very little control over when, how, and even whether they heard music to one where everything is available at any time, payment optional. That's the legacy of Napster, Kazaa, Grokster, and Limewire, the most well-known peer-to-peer (P2P) file-sharing sites. Not only did these sites permanently shift attitudes around music consumption, they are also largely responsible for the recorded music industry losing half its value in just three years—from $14.6 billion in 1999 to $6.3 billion in 2003.

After the arrival of the original Napster site in 1999, labels and publishers began lobbying Congress to take legislative action. Ultimately, it was the courts that would decide the fate of P2P services from Napster onward. Looking back, the music industry should thank Congress for punting to the judicial branch. Copyright owners have won a string of injunctions against and damages from P2P operators since Napster was KO'd in 2001. I'll get into much more detail about copyright enforcement in chapter 6, but suffice it to say that without P2P we wouldn't have Spotify. Whether you think that would be a good thing or not is your own business.

Online Music Goes Legitimate

I've heard plenty of people say that labels should have just done a deal with Napster rather than suing the site into oblivion. That's an easy position to take in hindsight. At the time, however, licensing P2P would have been next to impossible. First, the recorded music business was at that point almost entirely powered by physical sales. You can see why there was reluctance to abandon a lucrative revenue model for one that wasn't just unproven—it simply didn't exist. The phrase "paradigm shift" gets tossed around so much that it has become a cliché, but in my view, P2P satisfies the criteria.

Let's recap: In 1999, there were six major labels. There were a great many more independents, not to mention thousands of music publishers. Neither the operators of the P2P sites nor their music business counterparts were in a position to come to anything resembling a consensus on how to establish a compensation structure for this new form of distribution. It didn't take too long to get there, all things considered. A business model was eventually established for digital music, first with download stores like iTunes and later with on-demand streaming services such as Spotify. The music economy is now based on access, an idea that finds its roots in the P2P revolution.

You Win Some, YouTube Some

I'll talk a lot more about user-upload sites in chapter 6, which looks at copyright enforcement online. I bring it up here because one such site, YouTube, has become a major player in digital music. As you may know, YouTube operates under a part of the law known as the Digital Millennium Copyright Act (DMCA), which was passed in 1998. Among other things, this legislation gives online service providers what's known as a "safe harbor" from copyright liability for infringements committed by users. That is, if the service expeditiously responds to takedown notices sent by the rights holder for each incident of infringement by removing or disabling access to said material.

These days, YouTube licenses much of its music content from labels and publishers. That doesn't make them besties. Rights holders complain that the fees they receive from YouTube are considerably lower than on-demand audio services like Spotify. The major music companies say that YouTube's safe harbor forces them to accept smaller fees or else play "whack-a-mole" with notice and takedown. YouTube counters that in 2017 alone, it paid one billion dollars to rights holders from advertising around videos featuring music.

That's a lot of money because YouTube gets a lot of visitors. Many go there specifically for music. YouTube's userbase dwarfs Spotify's (800 million versus 100 million users).[8] Rights holders say this means YouTube should be paying them a great deal more money. What this tells me is that YouTube and the DMCA safe harbors will continue to be a sore point for however long it takes to address these issues in new legislation. Efforts to persuade Congress to update the DMCA have thus far fallen flat, though this may be changing. Depending on where things end up, we may see another shift in how music is consumed. And if not, you can post a video rant about it. Just make sure you have the rights to any music you use.

NEW MARKETS, NEW METHODS

For much of the music industry's history, the path to the marketplace for creators was narrow. Artists and songwriters had few options but to sign with a music company in order to see their work go beyond their hometowns. It could be that a lot of great music never had a chance to be heard. These days, a lot of music is ignored due to the sheer amount available. Still, I think I prefer the way things are now because I like the increase in options. And that includes different ways of getting music into the world.

In the early 2000s, Radiohead and Nine Inch Nails experimented with "pay what you want" direct download schemes, which helped pave the way for sites like Bandcamp, which gives artists flexibility over access and pricing. Other user-upload sites such as Soundcloud have helped launch the careers of any number of producers in Electronic Dance Music (EDM) and hip-hop, including Kascade and Chance the Rapper. Some artists who gain attention online may end up doing deals with labels or publishers. Other times, they'll remain independent. Coming from a different era, I appreciate that they have the choice. Not every artist will be able to make a go of it without backing from a label or publishers, but at least it's possible.

The Internet forced the music industry to reconfigure its longstanding business models to meet the expectations of audiences who have come to expect "always on" access to music. Now that those business models actually exist, it means more opportunities for exploiting music copyrights. It also means greater challenges in collecting and delivering royalties. Frankly, it shouldn't mean that. Technology gives us new tools to track music consumption for the purposes of payment, and it also gives us the ability to keep accurate records on who needs to be paid. So what's the problem? Let's start with a lack of transparency. It's true that payouts for artists in many instances are low, but it's not always easy to understand why. A lot of it comes down to the information about who owns and authored the music. Paying people properly requires knowing who to pay, which I'll discuss further in chapter 7.

THERE IS NO PAUSE BUTTON

The shift to digital affected various industry participants in different ways. For example, songwriters were particularly impacted by the unbundling of the album format. Before iTunes, if you wrote a song that ended up on a platinum-selling album but it wasn't the hit driving sales, you'd still make 9.1 cents per copy sold. That all changed when online services began offering music track by track. That's just one example. There are many others. As I get back to the specific rules around sound recordings and musical works, I encourage you to keep in mind that things can and do change. That's actually a good thing because in music change means opportunity.

4

MUSICAL WORKS AND COPYRIGHT EXCLUSIVITIES

IT ALL STARTS WITH THE SONG

In our current era, we tend to think of individual pieces of music as "tracks," which is to say, recordings by a band or featured artist. However, as previously noted, sound recordings embody underlying compositions that have an entirely separate copyright. In fact, compositions are the basis for music copyright, period. This is because everything starts with the song.

Think about it: Without musical compositions or lyrics, there would be nothing for recording artists to perform. Even improvised music is a kind of real-time composition. That's why it's important to understand the exclusive rights that attach to musical works. Remember, when a songwriter comes up with a tune or lyrics and "fixes" them in a tangible form—whether it's notes on paper or a recording that embodies the composition—it automatically falls within copyright. The songwriter or their publisher may choose to register the musical work with the U.S. Copyright Office to qualify for certain benefits, such as statutory damages in the case of infringement (for more information on copyright registration, see chapter 7). But whether or not the musical work is registered, it is nonetheless covered by copyright, so long as it is a work of original expression.

At this point, it makes sense to go back to our list of exclusive rights to see how they line up with musical works. As you recall from chapter 1, those exclusivities are:

Reproduction/Distribution
Public Performance
Adaptation/Derivative Works
Public Display

Having a sense of how musical works function within each of these buckets is key to understanding the complexities of what's known as music publishing. At its core, music publishing is about who gets to exploit musical works and under what conditions. If you understand this, you are in a much better position to fathom the rest of music copyright. In some instances, the licensing of musical works falls under a government framework, with rate setting overseen by federal judges (with the process and venue for determinations based on the type of use). Other types of licenses, such as the use of a composition in an audiovisual work (known as "synchronization"), require direct negotiation with the owner(s) of the musical work.

Musical works often have multiple coauthors and copublishers. This can make licensing—the process of obtaining permission and determining compensation—a real challenge. That's because there isn't a single authoritative repository containing information on who controls what portion of the world's songs. Knowing where to go to obtain a license is hardly intuitive. Nor is it simple to track down royalties for every type of use. By learning how copyright exclusivities interact with musical works, you'll have a leg up in the world of music publishing.

REPRODUCTION/DISTRIBUTION OF MUSICAL WORKS

As described in chapter 1, the right to reproduce a work is the most fundamental exclusivity granted to authors. It is the "copy" in copyright, and it applies to all types of original expression. With musical works, the right to make a copy has a bearing on sound recordings that embody underlying compositions—that's any music recording that you can hear.

Again, everything starts with the song. Once a musical work has been fixed in a tangible form and made available by its composer(s), any performer can record a version, provided they—or their label—pay a so-called compulsory royalty.

The requirement that users of underlying compositions pay a government-set rate is what makes this license compulsory. (You may also hear the term "statutory license," which means the same thing.) This is different from voluntary licenses, where parties come to terms among themselves. With compulsory licenses, it is not necessary to directly negotiate with the owner(s) of a musical work, though they can also be obtained via voluntary agreement. The basic point to remember is that a license is *always* required to make reproductions of musical works that aren't in the public domain. This is the case even if the sound recording embodying the musical work is given away for free. The compulsory license for the reproduction of musical works is more commonly known as a "mechanical" license.

You'll recall from chapter 3 that mechanical royalties came about as a response to player pianos (figure 4.1). Mechanical royalties have since been extended to cover more uses—essentially, any embodiment of a song that can be played back as audio via technical means. This applies to physical media such as LPs, CDs, and cassettes, as well as downloadable files and on-demand streaming. The idea is that all of these uses of musical works involve a reproduction and distribution of an underlying composition and therefore require permission and payment to the owner(s) of that composition.

THE MECHANICS OF MECHANICALS

In order to lawfully reproduce a musical work, you need to have secured a mechanical license. As of the time of this writing, the mechanical royalty rate for physical recordings (think CDs and LPs) and downloads is 9.1 cents for recordings of five minutes or less and 1.75 cents per minute (or fraction thereof) for songs longer than five minutes. The rates for ringtones are 24 cents per copy. You may occasionally hear mechanical royalties referred to as "penny rates"—this is due to the fact that they are calculated in cents rather than dollars. Rates are set by the

Figure 4.1. Player piano, circa 1910. *Source:* Antique Piano Shop, https://antiquepianoshop.com/restoration-process/1910-autopiano-player-piano/.

Copyright Royalty Board (CRB), a trio of federal judges who hear arguments and consider evidence from various parties before making a determination on rates to cover a period (typically five years).

Until a recent update to Section 115 of the Copyright Act, compulsory licensors were required to send a Notice of Intent (NOI) to at least *one* of the publishers no later than thirty days before making a reproduction/distribution (the publisher receiving the notice was responsible for paying royalties to any copublishers). With the passage of the Music Modernization Act (MMA) on October 11, 2018, this framework has been overhauled, including the standards by which compulsory royalties are set.

The Section 115 compulsory license also sets the rules for reporting to publishers and the distribution of royalties, which have also changed with the new law. Under the previous regime, if a user was unable to locate any of a song's publishers, they could file notice with the Copyright Office, which would publish the NOI in the case that the owner(s) came forward. Failure to comply meant the user of the musical work would be ineligible for the compulsory license and potentially liable for infringement. This system has been scrapped under the MMA. Going forward, mechanical licenses will be facilitated by the Mechanical Licensing Collective (MLC), which will also operate a database of information pertaining to the ownership of musical works. However, users of musical works may still negotiate permission and fees directly with a publisher or their designated agents. (Publishers often choose to license directly because the deals may include other rights and considerations.) The MMA also provides publishers and songwriters with an audit right, which they did not enjoy under the former framework.

Physical Media and "Controlled Compositions"

For physical media, such as LPs, cassettes, and CDs, mechanical royalties are paid by labels to publishers. The publishers then compensate the songwriters, typically according to a 50/50 split, whereby the writers receive half of the mechanical royalty collected. Until recently, this was also the case for downloads. With the MMA now law, operators of download services such as iTunes will be eligible to obtain mechanical licenses from the new collective (MLC), which will in turn deliver royalties to publishers. For physical media, labels will continue to pay publishers directly.

Where labels are responsible for compensating publishers, mechanical royalties may be negotiated downward under such schemes as "controlled composition." Under some artist contracts, performers who write their own songs are subject to caps on mechanical royalties imposed by their label. This can be a reduction of up to 75 percent of whatever the mechanical royalty rate is at the time of the contract's execution. Which means that even if the government rate increases, the label's royalty obligation remains the same for as long as the contract is in effect. Labels may also impose an aggregate cap on the number of artist-composed songs on which they'll pay mechanicals, typically ten to twelve songs. So if you write fourteen songs for a record, the label only pays you for ten. If you're a performing songwriter in a deal that includes controlled composition, it could also impact cowriters who aren't signed to your label. Collaborators (or their publishers) may reject the cap on mechanicals, in which case your label will deduct the difference in their earnings from *your* royalties, thereby further reducing what you're paid. What a business.

Mechanical Licensing and On-Demand Streaming

Outside the United States, it is common for mechanical royalties to be calculated as a percentage of the wholesale or retail price of the sound recording. U.S. labels have expressed interest in this model, as it would allow them to potentially pay less in mechanicals for discounted recordings. American publishers and songwriters have been less enthusiastic about such proposals. However, publishers and songwriters have accepted a percentage of revenue framework for streaming.

Early in the transition to digital, there was debate about whether interactive streaming—where users can choose the specific track or album—should implicate the mechanical royalty. For some time, there was nothing in federal statute that referenced this obligation. However, precedent existed in the form of agreements between the early streaming service Rhapsody and music industry trade groups including the Recording RIAA and the National Music Publishers Association (NMPA). Those agreements have been used as the basis for rate setting by the CRB.[1] With the passage of the MMA, there is now statutory confirmation that on-demand streaming services must obtain mechanical licenses. Let's take a closer look at what that means.

Spotify and similar services such as Apple Music are deemed interactive because of what they allow users to do with audio tracks. Unlike radio—AM/FM or digital—subscribers can choose exactly which songs or albums they want to listen to. You can make playlists, download tracks for offline listening (as long you're subscribed), and even share music with other users. The compulsory mechanical license allows Spotify and similar services to license the underlying compositions embodied in sound recordings for a predetermined fee. Whereas the mechanical royalty for physical media is priced per song, the rate for interactive streaming is calculated as a percentage of revenue from subscriptions and advertising.[2] Unlike physical media, which is paid by labels to publishers, streaming mechanicals have historically been paid by the services directly to the publishers, who compensate songwriters according to contract (typically 50 percent). Self-published songwriters often hire publishing administrators to collect and distribute their royalties (more on that later). Under the MMA, on-demand streaming services and download stores that avail themselves of the compulsory mechanical license will report usage and pay royalties to a collective established for this purpose.[3] This change to the mechanical licensing regime came about in part due to streaming services' failure to pay mechanical royalties to songwriters and publishers.

In 2015, publishers and songwriters took legal action against Spotify for alleged underpayment of mechanical royalties. Under then current law, there were certain requirements for obtaining a mechanical license. These included sending at least one publisher notification thirty days prior to making a reproduction and distribution of a musical work. If the user failed to do so, they'd need to come to an agreement with every publisher who controls any portion of the work. Not a simple task, given the number of writers and copublishers that can have interests in a single song. Making matters worse is the fact that splits may not be determined until well after the sound recordings embodying those works are widely distributed.

Spotify probably assumed it had the permissions it needed because it had licenses from the Harry Fox Agency (HFA), which had long acted as the mechanical licensing agent for the three major publishers (and many independents). HFA was owned by the publishers until 2015, when it was sold to the performing rights organization Society of European Stage Authors and Composers (SESAC). Although HFA is authorized to license a large number of musical works, its repertoire does not cover every song on a service like Spotify. Many independent publishers and self-published songwriters whose music is streamed on interactive services are not members of HFA. Publishers claimed that Spotify and other interactive services also failed to get licenses for certain songs that are in HFA's repertoire. In 2016, Spotify reached a reported $30 million settlement that included a promise to work with the publisher community to establish robust databases on musical works ownership. Parties soon determined that new legislation would best serve this goal.

The Music Modernization Act and Mechanicals

Among other things, the MMA changes how mechanical royalties are calculated, as well as the process for obtaining mechanical licenses. (The law also impacts sound recordings, which I will discuss in the next chapter.) Major updates to the Copyright Act don't come around very often and typically require compromise among the various copyright communities—including artists, songwriters, music companies, technology firms, and even archivists and librarians. This bill was no different.

The amendments to Section 115 of the Copyright Act within the MMA were seen by services as preferable to ongoing liability. Discussions began in earnest around the time that Spotify was preparing to become a publicly traded company. Corporate financiers were no doubt concerned that legal issues around Spotify's use of copyrights could negatively impact the initial public offering (IPO). So, in a rare display of unity, services like Apple Music, Amazon Music, and Spotify joined forces with the music publishers to push for a change in how musical works are licensed. First and foremost, the MMA eliminates the NOI process by establishing a blanket license for mechanicals used on digital services. Previously, licensing was done on a per-song basis—which, considering the large catalogs available on today's digital platforms, made for a very cumbersome and inefficient licensing process.

The MMA also updates how rates for mechanical licenses are determined. Now, Section 115 of the Copyright Act directs the CRB to consider free-market conditions when setting rates, which many publishers and songwriters believe will result in increased revenue for the use of their musical compositions. We'll see if that bears out. However, it's not always easy to set rates under the so-called willing buyer/willing standard, especially if there is no comparable market. The MMA allows parties to license directly, which could serve as benchmarks in CRB proceedings. But those direct deals happen under the shadow of the compulsory license, which sets the ceiling for rates. Chicken versus egg? More like snake eats tail.

The Mechanical Licensing Collective

The centerpiece of the music publishing portion of MMA is the creation of the MLC, which serves as a licensing body for the compulsory mechanical royalty. The MMA authorizes the Register of Copyrights for the U.S. Copyright Office to designate an organization to run the collective and issue blanket mechanical licenses. The law requires the MLC to create a publicly accessible repository of information on musical works ownership. This is a significant development.

The Copyright Office has determined that a consortium of publishers and songwriters—including the NMPA—will manage the operations of the MLC. The cost of operating the collective will be paid by services that use mechanical licenses. The MLC governing board includes ten publishers, four self-published songwriters, and three nonvoting advisers, including one representative for the digital services.

It is no small effort to pull together the information needed to populate an authoritative database on song authorship and ownership. The devil, as they say, is in the details, and musical works have plenty of those. Some observers claim the NMPA (which represents publishers, including the Big Three—Warner Chappell Music, Sony Music Publishing, and Universal Music Publishing Group) has little incentive to identify all the parties who are owed money because the law lets them divvy up unmatched royalties by market share after three years. Still, having a publicly available database on musical works ownership is a step in the right direction for transparency in the music industry.

Though much remains to be worked out, we have a general sense of how the MLC will operate. First off, the MLC's ability to issue blanket mechanical licenses will allow services to obtain bulk repertoire that matches to the sound recordings they have already licensed from record labels. Increased efficiency could result in more songs being licensed, which is good news for their writers and owners. The challenge will be matching usage as reported by services to every and all parties who control any portion of the compositions. Much effort is also needed to get songwriters signed up with the new collective.

There are still questions about how the MLC will fulfill its mandate, but we know what it *won't* be doing. The collective is prohibited from licensing anything beyond mechanicals (no performance royalties, no synchronizations, etc.). Licensors and licensees are still allowed to negotiate voluntary agreements, and major publishers are likely to do just that. Self-published songwriters are the MLC's prime demographic, but many of them already use services like Tunecore Music Publishing, Songtrust, or CD Baby to administer their publishing. If there are future editions of this book, I'll surely have something about whether the MMA/MLC solved any problems or if it was merely a black box bonanza for big publishers.

Cover Songs and User Uploads

There has been much confusion around artists covering songs on services like YouTube. Technically, cover artists need mechanical licenses, though it's rare that they go about getting them before posting a video. With covers, only the musical work is implicated—the newly recorded performance is its own copyright that belongs to the performer (or their label). In my view, music on YouTube is more like a synchronization (or sync) because it fixes a musical work in another medium (video). But YouTube—which is owned by Google—claims it doesn't need that type of license because it isn't making the synchronization but is simply hosting the audio-video. And so covers on YouTube are more or less treated like mechanicals.

Thankfully for all the bedroom strummers out there YouTube has direct deals with the major publishers (and many independents), which in theory "covers" covers. This means you can upload your ukulele performance of Slayer's "Raining Blood" with little chance of being sued. YouTube also has agreements with PROs such as ASCAP, BMI, and SESAC to cover the public performance. Let's now take a closer look.

PUBLIC PERFORMANCE OF MUSICAL WORKS

I've already given a history lesson on public performance of musical works. So now I'll focus on the overall framework for this exclusive right.

I'll also outline various arguments for retaining, modifying, or sunsetting the ASCAP and BMI consent decrees. And as is the case with mechanicals, the MMA changed how public performances rates are set, which I'll briefly describe.

How Performance Licenses Work

The public performance of musical works includes the use of underlying compositions on broadcast radio (AM/FM), digital radio (satellite radio, webcasting), and public establishments where music is played (concert halls, stadiums, clubs, bars, restaurants, hotel lobbies, etc.). By contrast, sound recordings have a limited performance right that applies only to digital radio. (I'll rant about that disparity more in the next chapter.)

Royalties from the performance of musical compositions are collected and distributed by PROs. In the United States that's ASCAP, BMI, SESAC, and a newer PRO called Global Music Rights (GMR). Of these organizations, only ASCAP and BMI are regulated by the government. Money from public performances for all forms of broadcasting and public venues are collected by the PROs and distributed to their member songwriters and publishers, typically according to a 50/50 split—half to the publisher(s) and half to the songwriter(s) according to the portions each party controls. The public performance of musical works generates a lot of money; BMI reported distributing more than $1 billion in royalties in 2015.[4] One reason this sector remains strong is that there are many places where music is performed publicly.

Any time an artist plays a song in a concert, it's a public performance of a musical work. The same goes for a DJ spinning prerecorded music. When a song is played on AM/FM or digital radio, that, too, is a public performance. It's also true of music heard at the gym, the grocery store, or your favorite dive bar. The definition of "public" in this context is any place where the general public is free to go—regardless of the number of people or whether there is an admission fee. That includes retail establishments, bars, restaurants, and hotels, in addition to concert venues and broadcast stations.[5]

Thanks to blanket licenses from PROs, it is not necessary to directly negotiate with copyright owners for permission to perform a song. PROs perform three basic functions:

1. Providing blanket licenses and collecting fees
2. Tracking public performances to calculate royalties
3. Distributing royalties to songwriter and publisher members

Fees vary based on the licensee's audience size, revenues, and how much music is performed. PROs use proprietary formulas to determine how royalties are apportioned; see chapter 8 for more details.

ADAPTATIONS/DERIVATIVE WORKS

Fun fact: Sound recordings are actually derivative works because they are always based on an underlying composition.[6] There are other kinds of musical works derivatives that can qualify for copyright protection. These, too, require permission from the owner(s) of the original copyright if the work is not in the public domain.

Section 106(2) of the Copyright Act defines a derivative work as

> a work based upon one or more preexisting works, such as a translation, musical arrangement, fictionalization, motion picture version, sound recording, art reproduction, abridgement, condensation, or any other form in which a work may be recast, transformed or adapted.[7]

A key question for derivative works is whether a transformation or adaptation is eligible for a separate copyright. As a general matter, the answer is yes. The 1909 Copyright Act established protections for derivative works, which was extended within the 1976 Act. However, these protections are subject to certain requirements. Let's review those criteria.

Copyright-Eligible Derivative Works

If a work that is adapted is still under copyright, permission must be granted by the owner of that work. There is no compulsory or statutory license in this part of copyright, so the party making the derivative or adaptation must negotiate directly with the copyright owner or their agent for the right to do so. However, if a work is in the public domain, no permission is required.

For a new creation based on an existing work to qualify for separate copyright protection, it must satisfy the statutory requirements for derivative works, which are twofold and apply to copyrighted works as well as those in the public domain:

- the new work must borrow from an existing work to be considered derivative, and
- the new work must recast, transform, or adapt the original work.

This is where the originality requirement comes into play. In music, it is common for performers and arrangers to include stylistic flourishes that may not be enough to justify a new copyright. If, for example, you covered "Eleanor Rigby" by the Beatles in a heavy metal style but made no significant alterations or transformations to the melody and lyrics, you would not be able to claim a new musical work copyright.

However, if you *record* your heavy metal performance of "Eleanor Rigby" you have created a new sound copyright distinct from the Beatles's cut. All you need is a compulsory license to reproduce and distribute the underlying composition embodied in your new version and you're free to blow our collective minds. But (there's always a but) if you were to add elements of original creativity that significantly transforms the underlying composition, you may be able to claim a separate copyright for the new composition as a derivative work. In which case, you'd be the owner of both the sound recording *and* the new musical work based on the existing composition.

So who decides what is or isn't significant when it comes to original expression added to an existing work? There are gray areas in terms of what qualifies as transformative, and it often comes down to courts to decide. Subtle variations in a song's arrangement or a minor lyrical change or aside may not qualify. Using elements of an existing work in an entirely new creation is more likely to be transformative. It's important to remember that copyright protection for derivative works covers *only* the portions of a new work where there is original expression. Specifically, Section 103(b) of the Copyright Act states:

> The copyright in a compilation or a derivative work extends only to the material contributed by the author of such a work, as distinguished from the preexisting material employed in the work, and does not imply any exclusive right in the preexisting material. The copyright in such work is independent of, and does not affect or enlarge the scope, duration, ownership, or subsistence of, any copyright protection in the preexisting material.

In some instances, permission is not required to alter an original work. I already mentioned works in the public domain that are no longer protected by copyright. Another possibility is that the adaptation or transformation is a fair use. The fair use doctrine is a part of copyright law that allows for certain uses of existing works, such as excerpts for the purposes of education or criticism. (Fair use will be covered in more detail in chapter 6.) Keep in mind that fair use is an "affirmative defense," which means a use isn't considered noninfringing until action is brought and the user invokes fair use as a defense. At which point, a judge will consider evidence specific to that use and render a decision based on criteria that I'll enumerate later.

Derivative Work Categories

There are several types of work that the law considers derivative. Not all of them apply to music, but some do, so let's have a quick look.

Editorial Revisions. If this book ends up in a second printing that includes new information that is not in the original edition, that would be considered an editorial revision and therefore eligible for a separate derivative copyright. This would apply to music compositions if a composer or songwriter published an expanded version of a work that includes additional verses or musical elements.

Fictionalizations. Think of turning a nonfiction work into a fictional book, movie, or show. An example would be the documentary about the Glorious Ladies of Wrestling, which Netflix adapted into a scripted series. I suppose you could do that with musical compositions, so I'll look forward to reading your graphic novel based on *Tales from Topographic Oceans* by Yes. That's nonfiction, right?[8]

Dramatizations. Such as adapting J. K. Rowling's Harry Potter novels into a movie, or taking a book, story, or film and adapting it for a stage production, like *The Lion King* Broadway musical.

Translations. This is like when a book written in French is translated to English. Or when the song "Der Kommissar" by German pop star Falco was given an English-language makeover by After the Fire. With literary and lyrical translations, there is often some original creativity involved, so they too may be eligible for a separate copyright.

Translations into a New Medium. This is where we can place sound recordings that embody musical works. As previously noted, sound recordings containing music are derivative "translations" into a new medium, as they involve a performance based on the underlying composition.

Abridgments and Condensations. This applies to situations where a work is modified by making it shorter, such as an abridged version of a novel. In music, abridgements are most common with classical suites.

PUBLIC DISPLAY

This exclusivity is quite narrow when it comes to music and tends to only come up for well-known songs and writers. Here we're talking about lyrics (which are a part of musical compositions) publicly displayed in other media like lyrics featured onscreen in a movie or TV show.

WHERE IS MY MONEY?

Writing a song is often easier than getting paid for its exploitation. I'll get into greater detail regarding music licensing in chapter 8, but I wanted to touch on a few areas of importance in terms of how songwriters earn revenue. Ownership determines how you get paid, how much, and how often, so it's important to understand these basics.

Music Publishers

If a songwriter is self-published, they are eligible to receive 100 percent of the royalty on songs they composed themselves. So why would a songwriter work with a music publisher if it means giving up at least half of their mechanical and performance royalties? Well, music publishers have expertise, reach, and leverage, which can help when it comes to negotiating favorable deals and chasing down payments. They are also versed in market rates for various types of uses, including those outside of statutory or compulsory frameworks (synchronizations come immediately to mind). Publishers sometimes enter copublishing arrangements to deal with rights management and royalties in other territories, as foreign publishers know their local market and are better positioned to track usage. Just be sure to check the fine print in your contract to ensure that any copublishing or subpublishing arrangements make sense for you.

Many publishing deals are based on 50/50 splits postrecoupment. In some instances, publishers will offer advances to support songwriters in the creation of new works. Whether you sign with a publisher or go it alone, it's always advisable to have a qualified attorney review any contracts, as it can be hard to know whether the terms on offer reflect the value of the work(s) being licensed.

Payment for Public Performance

For performance rights, the two biggest PROs—ASCAP and BMI—will accept any songwriter or publisher as a member. (SESAC and GMR are invite only.) As previously noted, PROs pay publishers and writers according to a 50/50 split; if a songwriter is unsigned and has no cowriters, they can register as the publisher to get the full amount owed. PROs also have reciprocal agreements with global collecting societies to capture royalties for performances outside the United States. Songwriters and publishers may also be able to register directly with foreign PROs, which in some cases is more efficient and can reduce administrative deductions.

Payment for Mechanicals

Mechanical royalties are more challenging to manage. Remember, every time an underlying composition is reproduced/distributed it implicates the mechanical right. Individual songwriters are ill equipped to track down mechanical royalties owed in a global music marketplace, which is one reason songwriters may choose to sign with a publisher. These days, however, there are any number of "publishing administration" services that will collect mechanical and other royalties on your behalf. Songwriters who do a certain volume of business but want to retain their copyrights may also choose a service like Kobalt to administer their mechanicals. And let's not forget the MLC, which aims to serve independent and unaffiliated songwriters who sign up with the collective.

Payment for Synchronizations

Synchronizations (licensing of musical works to film, television, advertising, video games, etc.) exist apart from any compulsory or statutory framework. These uses are "free-market" negotiations wherein fees are based on any number of factors, from the type of placement to audience size to the popularity of the song being licensed. Both the musical work and the sound recording are required for "syncing" to video and are licensed separately. A very well-known song performed by a celebrated act is more likely to command greater fees than a work by an up-and-coming artist. A song that has been licensed a ton may see its value diminish over time. A "must-have" song gives the owner(s) more leverage to demand higher fees. Music that is considered replaceable will fetch less. Payment for synchronizations comes directly from the licensee or their designated agent based on each agreement; common fee structures and terms are described in chapter 8.

JOINT WORKS

In many cases, there are multiple authors of a musical composition. These days, it's more unusual for a hit song to have only one writer or publisher. Songwriters can transfer their ownership in whatever percentage, which complicates matters further. Often, big-name performers who had nothing to do with a song's composition will be "cut in" to the publishing in exchange for recording the song. All of which is to say that the universe of musical works authorship ownership can be devilishly complex.

The U.S. Copyright Act defines a joint work as one having been created by two or more authors whose intent is that their individual contributions are part of a unified whole (you can think of lyrics and music as being interdependent but unified components of a song). When band members write a song together, they are often considered joint works, though the band would be responsible for determining the percentages of ownership based on individual members' contributions. Determining ownership percentages can be tricky, but it's important to do. Copyright registration is also a good idea. Courts consider information from Copyright Office applications and registrations to identify authors for the purpose of settling disputes. If a claimant is not identified as such, there is a higher burden in proving coauthorship.

There are instances where components of a song are not considered joint works. For example, if there is a preexisting poem that is later put to music, the individual copyrights (lyrics and music) may remain separate as the song would be considered a derivative of the original poem. For true joint works, Section 201(a) of the Copyright Act sets equal, undivided interests unless the authors specify otherwise. Meaning, if I write the bulk of a song but you contribute 10 percent of its copyrightable elements, the default legal position would be 50/50. However, songwriters are free to enumerate ownership in any percentage so long as their agreement is put in writing.

Licensing Joint Works

Since the law recognizes coauthors as having equal, undivided interests, joint owners of copyright have the right to use the work or give permission for others to do so. A recognized joint owner can license the entirety of a work without authorization from any coauthors. Which means that the song we wrote together can be licensed by either you or me without either of us having to get permission from the other. If you want to license the song for use in a Trump campaign video, you may do so even over my objections. (However, I am entitled to receive fees or royalties for such a use based on whatever portion of the song I own.) The exception is that neither of us can offer an exclusive license to the coowned work, so I could turn around and license that same song to a different candidate. A cowriter or coowner of a joint work who licenses it for exploitation has the obligation to account to their cowriters and coowners.

CONCLUSION

At this point, it should be clear that musical works (aka songs, or underlying compositions) have a high degree of complexity that is only becoming more challenging to manage due to the global Internet. Addressing these issues requires better systems to identify all parties with an interest in a musical work. This can mean legislation like the MMA or private market solutions. Copyright reform is a slow and often agonizing process, and in the meantime, there is still a business to stay on top of. My hope is that you now have a better understanding of the finer points of musical works exploitation. In the next chapter I'll cover how copyright exclusivities apply to sound recordings. (Don't worry, it's much shorter.)

5

SOUND RECORDINGS AND COPYRIGHT EXCLUSIVITIES

PERFORMANCES FIXED IN A TANGIBLE MEDIUM

Now we'll look at how sound recordings are exploited and the various rules and exceptions that govern their use. First, a reminder that sound recordings are performances "fixed in a tangible medium." If a band plays a song and nobody records it, that performance isn't fixed and therefore ineligible for copyright protections—there's no recording made. As is the case with musical works, the basic eligibility requirement for sound recording copyrights is fixation.

For sound recordings, "tangible medium" refers to any media that can be played back, such as audio tape or computer hard drive. Exploitation of sound recordings happens when the recording is reproduced, distributed, or performed as a noninteractive digital transmission—all of which requires a license of specific permission from the owner(s) of that recording. Fees for such uses are either negotiated directly (in the case of the distribution right) or arrived at through government rate setting (such as noninteractive digital public performances of sound recordings).

To simplify: Physical, download, and on-demand uses of sound recordings require direct negotiation with the copyright owner or their designated agent. Noninteractive "digital radio" falls under a statutory/

compulsory license administered by the nonprofit royalties collective SoundExchange (figure 5.1). Okay, so maybe simple isn't the right word.

Sound recordings enjoy many of the same protections as musical works, but the rights aren't perfectly analogous between the two copyrights. For example, although there is a public performance right for both musical works and sound recordings, the sound recording right is—in the United States, anyway—limited to digital noninteractive transmissions. This means only Internet, satellite, and cable radio are required by U.S. law to pay royalties to performing artists (think singers and musicians) and sound copyright owners (most often labels, but sometimes artists). So-called terrestrial radio broadcasters (over-the-air AM/FM stations) are exempt from paying performance royalties on sound recordings.

Likewise, there is no royalty for sound recordings used in public establishments, as is the case for musical works. But that's getting a bit ahead of ourselves. Let's begin as we did in the previous chapter on musical works by taking a look at which exclusivities apply to sound recordings and the frameworks that govern their exploitation. My explanations will be shorter than the previous chapter, as the exclusivities are more or less similar between musical works and sound recordings. I will, however, zero in on the exceptions, particularly the aforementioned lack of a broadcast performance right for sound recordings.

The primary exclusivities that apply to sound recordings are:

Reproduction/Distribution
Public Performance
Adaptation/Derivative Works
Master License (synchronization)

THE REPRODUCTION/DISTRIBUTION RIGHT AND SOUND RECORDINGS

Say you're in a band that is laying down tracks at a local studio. You record a batch of songs for your debut album. Who owns these recordings? You and your fellow performers do. That is, unless you transfer ownership to a third party such as a record label. And why would you do that? Most likely for an advance and the opportunity for your tracks to be more widely distributed and marketed. In the predigital era, signing with a label was pretty much the only path to the marketplace for artists. That's because the creation, manufacturing, and distribution of sound recordings was cost prohibitive for the vast majority of musicians. Back then, making a sonically competitive album required considerable investment. So did promoting it. A label's production and marketing spend became part of an artist's "recoupable costs," which meant that even some well-known artists have yet to receive royalties from sales of their recordings.

The DIY Approach

These days, pretty much anyone can record a piece of music and distribute it online for free or at nominal cost. Platforms like Soundcloud and YouTube allow anyone to upload their music and, depending on the terms of service, monetize plays or downloads. There are also any number of indie aggregators like CD Baby, Tunecore, and Distrokid that will distribute your recordings to global digital stores and streaming services relatively inexpensively. Some of these "indie aggregators" have an initial setup charge and an annual fee to keep your recordings in digital storefronts. Others charge a percentage of royalties from downloads and plays, with a small to nonexistent initial setup charge and no restock fee. Which framework is best for you probably depends on how often your music is downloaded or streamed. An up-front fee plus yearly restock charge means that you'll have to do a certain amount of business to "recoup" your investment on a first-time and recurring basis. However, in this scenario, you get to keep 100 percent of royalties owed. Some aggregators may not have a setup or restock fee but will take a slice of whatever royalties are generated from downloads or plays for as long as your music is made available.

If your recordings tend to be popular, it may make more sense to pay a flat fee so that you keep all of your royalties after setup costs. If your sales and streams are more modest, a percentage of royalties may be a better choice. (Setup, restocking, and percentage fees vary; be sure to look closely at an aggregator's terms to determine what best suits your needs.) Keep in mind that micropennies from streaming take longer to add up than royalties from downloads. But my overall point stands: distributing your recordings globally is far easier and much less costly than in previous eras.

What Labels Can Offer

Just because your recordings are available is no guarantee that anyone will hear them. This is another reason some artists choose to sign with labels with the resources to promote their work. A 2014 study by the international major label trade organization, the International Federation of the Phonographic Industry, found that breaking an artist in the biggest music markets can cost anywhere from $500,000 to $2 million.[1] There are, of course, recording artists doing brisk business without a label. For example, Chance the Rapper has remained fiercely independent even as his profile reaches or exceeds major-backed talent. A successful independent artist will at some point need to build a team to manage the activities that would normally fall to a label or hire third parties to cover some of those bases. This can include partnerships to assist with distribution while the artist retains full ownership of their sound copyrights.

Maybe you still want to sign with a label. There are perfectly valid reasons for doing so; just keep in mind that music companies with promotional muscle and that can offer bigger advances are looking to sign artists who already have some traction in the marketplace. Which means your first goal is the same no matter what: to generate interest in your music. Accomplishing this can look different from artist to artist or even genre to genre. For example, an EDM artist's approach to building buzz is probably not the same as a bluegrass act. The best labels know how to cater to these communities. Just as there are fans of individual artists, there are fans of labels, especially in the independent sector. I know I've bought plenty of albums simply because they came out on a trusted imprint like Drag City, Merge Records, or Tzadik. And like many of my generation, I still associate certain legacy artists with their labels, like Bob Dylan (Columbia), Led Zeppelin (Atlantic), or the Beatles (Capitol).

Another reason to sign with a label is that they are pros at getting recorded music to the masses. Majors, for example, own multiple millions of actively distributed audio tracks, and their control over much of the modern distribution pipeline means that independents often use major-owned companies to physically and digitally distribute their recordings around the world. In this way, major labels have maintained their leverage in today's music ecosystem. They are also able to get their hands on revenue streams formerly off-limits to labels, which can be a double-edged sword.

Today, most major artist contracts (and some independent label agreements) are so-called 360-degree deals, which means the label will take percentages of revenue unrelated to the recordings, such as tour grosses, merch sales, or sponsorships and endorsements. An argument in favor of 360 deals is that, with additional skin in the game, labels are incentivized to more aggressively promote their artists. An argument against them is that, even where a label doesn't take an active role in development, they still get ancillary income from commercial activity beyond album sales or streams. Although 360 deals are now an industry standard, for these reasons they remain controversial.

Artist Services

Another option for today's artists is licensing their recordings to "artist services" companies, whereby a third party enjoys the exclusive right to reproduce and distribute sound recordings for a period of time or takes a percentage of revenue generated by the recordings. Such companies may also handle other activities such as management, marketing and promotion, synchronization and master use licenses, or even branding and merchandise. Deals can look different from project to project, so it's a good idea to work with an experienced music attorney when considering such an arrangement. Still, this full-service approach is becoming increasingly popular due to its flexibility and the fact that the artist keeps their copyrights.

PUBLIC PERFORMANCE AND SOUND RECORDINGS

In the United States, the performance right for sound recordings is limited to noninteractive digital uses only. This means Internet, satellite, and cable radio are all required to pay royalties for playing records on their services. Over-the-air AM/FM radio, however, is exempted from this obligation. It's a deeply unfair part of copyright law. The lack of a performance right on so-called terrestrial radio not only deprives American artists and labels of revenue but also distorts the global marketplace for sound recordings due to the lack of a reciprocal right between the United States and other countries. It puts noninteractive digital services at a competitive disadvantage, as these entities pay labels and performers as well as publishers and songwriters (AM/FM radio in the United States only pays on publishing). When you consider that the rest of the developed world has a terrestrial performance right, it's easy to see how this disparity warps the global market for music. Can you think of another product, good, or service that the United States would give away on the world stage with no expectation of remuneration? The terrestrial radio exemption has frustrated progress in streamlining music copyright overall—it's hard to have a conversation about parity when one sector pays nothing.

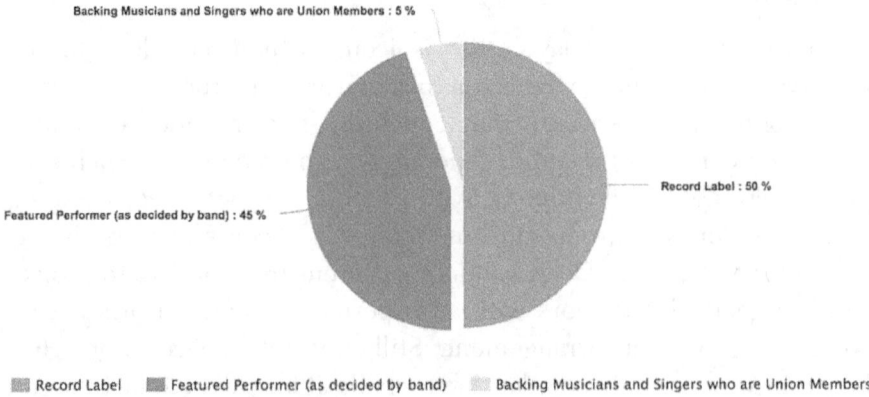

Figure 5.1. SoundExchange royalty splits.

How the Digital Performance Right for Sound Recordings Works

Under the statutory license established by Congress in 1995, noninteractive digital music services pay royalties to the nonprofit Sound-

SOUND RECORDINGS AND COPYRIGHT EXCLUSIVITIES 63

Exchange, which then pays artists and labels separately. SoundExchange takes a modest administrative fee of 4.9 percent and also makes a further deduction of 5 percent from the featured artists' share that goes to the musician unions Screen Actors Guild—American Federation of Television and Radio Artists (SAG-AFTRA) and the American Federation of Musicians (AFM), who in turn distribute this pool of money to union-backing musicians and vocalists (figure 5.1). The splits under the statutory license for sound recordings are as follows:

- 50 percent to the sound recording owner (typically the label, but it can be the artist)
- 45 percent to the featured performer (if a band, members can work out how to apportion this revenue)
- 5 percent to union background singers and musicians

Rates for the statutory license are set by a trio of federal judges overseen by the legislative branch. These judges are collectively known as the Copyright Royalty Board (CRB), the same crew that sets mechanical royalty rates. In proceedings, parties are able to present evidence before the judges regarding what they believe the rate should be. It doesn't always go smoothly. One thing that has frustrated rate setting under the statutory license is the lack of a comparable market to use as a benchmark. For example, the CRB can't use terrestrial radio as a proxy as there is no U.S. performance right for AM/FM. To use interactive streaming involves subtracting the value of the on-demand service on a per-subscriber basis. International rights aren't an option for reasons of jurisdiction. Perhaps this is why the statute permits direct deals between services and rights holders, as judges can consider fees from such agreements as benchmarks.

It's easy enough to sign up with SoundExchange as a performer, and all artists are encouraged to do so. Why? Because unless you have a direct deal with a service, it's the only way to get paid. I'll describe the ins and outs of registering with SoundExchange in chapter 8.

SOUND RECORDINGS AS DERIVATIVE WORKS

As mentioned in the previous chapter, sound recordings are already derivative works because they are always based on an underlying composition. It is also possible to make a derivative work out of existing sound recordings. Sample and remix artists do this all the time, but they don't always follow the law. Remember, making a derivative work requires permission from both the owners of the sound recordings and the musical works used. (As previously noted, sometimes permission is not required to make a derivative work. The fair use doctrine is a part of copyright law that allows for certain uses of existing works and is covered in chapter 6).

MASTER USE LICENSES (SYNCHRONIZATION)

To use a sound recording in another form of media like a television show, motion picture, advertisement, or video game requires permission from the owner of that sound recording. This is typically referred to as a "master license," but you may also hear it referred to as a "sync license." Technically, the latter applies to musical works, but the use scenario is pretty much the same. Master licenses (as well as synchronizations) are examined in more detail in chapter 8, where I'll describe how permissions and fees are negotiated for the use of sound recordings in other media. If you're a recording artist or sound copyright owner, this will be useful information, as the market for master uses continues to grow.

CONCLUSION

Overall, the exclusivities that attach to sound recordings are similar to those that apply to musical works. However, as you are now aware, sound recordings are prevented from generating revenue in certain parts of the American marketplace, such as prerecorded performances on AM/FM radio and live or prerecorded performances in public venues. For decades, artists, labels, and their advocates have pushed for a public performance right for sound recordings used on over-the-air radio, but thus far Congress has failed to pass legislation to do so. This is one of the more glaring inconsistencies in all of music copyright. Closing the terrestrial radio loophole would go a long way toward establishing a more rational system and greater parity between the exclusivities enjoyed by musical works and sound recordings. It is my hope that this unfair exemption is eliminated in federal legislation. Getting this done will require artists, labels, fans, and music services to make the case to Congress to do away with inequity once and for all.

6

COPYRIGHT ENFORCEMENT, SAFE HARBORS, AND FAIR USE

I've already touched on how Internet-based technologies have reshaped the music industry, with debates about online copyright enforcement looming large in the transition from physical to digital media. Now, I'll return to the topic with specific attention paid to the legal and policy response. This means another look at the grandaddy of file-sharing services, Napster, and the many sites it spawned. I'll also describe lawsuits against individual downloaders and legislative attempts to curb piracy. Next, I'll cover the specific rules governing notice and takedown for user-upload services. Last, I'll zero in on fair use as an "affirmative defense" against copyright infringement claims. And then I'll need a nap (ster).

THE P2P SHOT HEARD AROUND THE WORLD

Napster was created by computer programmer and college student Shawn Fanning in 1999. The original site allowed users' computers to access each other's audio files, with a straightforward search function that delivered instant results (even if downloads seemingly took forever on dial-up). The service grew rapidly: 150,000 people were signed up four months after release; within a year Napster had 26.4 million users, peaking at close to 80 million.

As Napster's popularity exploded, some well-known musicians spoke out, including Lars Ulrich of Metallica,[1] who in 2000 testified before Congress on the impacts of Napster (which has since become a fully licensed interactive streaming service).[2] Ulrich received harsh blowback from fans, with some pointing out how Metallica's initial popularity was boosted through the trading of bootleg cassettes, which the band did little to discourage. Ulrich wasn't the only one singled out: Napster users criticized other big-name performers as being rich and out of touch and accused labels of ripping off fans and artists alike (figure 6.1).

Some artists saw the original Napster as a useful platform for promotion—in 2000, Limp Bizkit inked an $18 million deal for the P2P service to promote a series of concerts by the band.[3] Obviously, not all music creators had that kind of leverage. For the most part, superstar artists and major labels were better positioned to survive the sudden shift from fans purchasing physical media to downloading music for free. Other musicians struggled to make up for dwindling label advances by constant touring, which is not always profitable and can come with high personal costs.

Smaller rights holders were also hit hard, with many independent labels, publishers, and distributors liquidating assets and closing shop. A court injunction forced the original Napster network to shut down in July 2001, but other file-sharing platforms like Kazaa, Gnutella, and Grokster soon emerged. In time, these services too would be knocked out by record industry lawsuits. The arrival of iTunes in early 2001 helped the industry establish a revenue model for digital music, yet piracy remained a huge concern for artists, songwriters, labels, and publishers for the remainder of the decade and beyond.

THE ERA OF ENDLESS LITIGATION

The International Federation of the Phonographic Industry (IFPI) blamed digital piracy for a 30 percent decline in recorded music revenue between 2004 and 2009.[4] Such steep losses may be why labels' legal divisions also chose to go after individual downloaders. In roughly

Figure 6.1. Lars Ulrich of Metallica testifies before Congress, July 11, 2000. *Source:* Kerrang, https://www.kerrang.com/features/metallica-vs-napster-the-lawsuit-that-redefined-how-we-listen-to-music/.

this same period, the recording industry filed lawsuits against some thirty thousand individuals, including children, grandparents, educators, and the deceased.[5] The first such lawsuit to go to trial involved an unemployed single mother who was slapped with $222,000 in damages for sharing twenty-four songs on Kazaa.[6]

As you might expect, this led to a mountain of bad publicity. The Recording Industry Association of America (RIAA) claimed such aggressive moves were a necessary deterrent, with then general counsel Cary Sherman claiming that "enforcement is a tough love form of education."[7] The lawsuits had no observable impact on Internet users' behavior, however, and the RIAA lost as many cases as they won. Artists whose music was pirated complained that they never saw a cent from even those prosecutions that were successful.[8] Eventually, the RIAA abandoned its legal campaign against individual downloaders and focused instead on technology companies that facilitate infringement. One suspected reason for the shift in strategy is that the labels were spending too much on legal fees; the head of litigation for Sony in 2007 called the RIAA campaign a "money pit" in sworn testimony.[9]

Infringement Goes Mega

The RIAA continues to scour the web for unlicensed uses of major label recordings. Some of the old enemies are still around: sites like Pirate Bay and others continue to provide links to unauthorized music downloads, often from locations beyond legal jurisdiction. In the late 2000s, the RIAA went after "locker" sites like Megaupload, which allowed pirates to upload various media and share link-based access with millions of Internet users (figure 6.2).[10] In January 2012, Megaupload mastermind Kim Dotcom found himself the target of a military-style raid when seventy armed police, including an antiterrorism squad, stormed his New Zealand mansion at the behest of U.S. authorities. Dotcom later settled with local forces for an undisclosed sum and continues to fight extradition to America.[11] Megaupload was one of several locker services that allowed uploaders to share links with anyone; many have chosen to cease operations or limit functionality due to liability concerns. Other lockers, such as those operated by Apple and Google, have been licensed by labels and publishers because they don't allow

Figure 6.2. Megaupload notice of government seizure.

sharing between users. However, with the proliferation of on-demand subscription services like Spotify, lockers have diminished in popularity and are no longer a primary target of music industry lawsuits.

Rip It Good

The latest target for major labels are companies that offer so-called stream ripping technology. Such sites and apps let users digitally extract audio and video from streaming platforms (regardless of whether the original upload was licensed). Labels represented by RIAA have successfully shut down a handful of stream ripping services, either through court action or the threat of court action, with "contributory copyright infringement" serving as the legal basis. Yet the issue remains unsettled: a Russian stream ripping company, FLVTO.biz, has petitioned the Supreme Court to take up its case based on an argument that the lower courts lacked jurisdiction to shutter the service.[12] Labels continue to rack up impressive wins in litigation against technology companies. In late 2020, the Eastern District of Virginia upheld a ruling that found Internet service provider Cox Communications liable for infringing music copyrights to the tune of $1 billion in damages.[13] Plenty to pay the lawyers and maybe even some leftover for artists.

LEGISLATIVE EFFORTS TO COMBAT PIRACY

In October 2011, members of the U.S. House of Representatives introduced a piece of legislation called the Stop Online Piracy Act, or SOPA. The bill attempted to frustrate Americans' access to foreign websites that traffic in the unauthorized distribution of intellectual property, including music. Well intentioned and enjoying support from a wide swath of the music sector, the legislation nevertheless failed to become law. I was involved in the highly contentious debates around SOPA, and I feel like they aged me by at least ten years. I suppose enough time has passed that I can summarize the events without feeling *too* triggered.

The goal of SOPA—to make it more difficult for rogue foreign websites to profit from the mass theft of U.S. intellectual property—not only remains worthwhile but also falls squarely within Congress's mandate to craft laws around copyright. However, there were concerns about unintended consequences stemming from its core provisions. Technologists and app developers felt that the overly broad language in the bill could stifle innovation. And free speech advocates and even some copyright creators worried about legitimate expression getting caught in SOPA's enforcement net.

To me, the SOPA debate should have been about U.S. law enforcement's capacity to address far-flung copyright infringement and whether its remedies were appropriately tailored. Instead, it was an aggressive attempt by some in the entertainment industries to ram undercooked legislation through Congress with little to no input from affected parties, including musicians. The tragedy of SOPA's spectacular fail is that Congress is now wary of wading into online copyright enforcement due to intense blowback from constituents and certain stakeholders. Had the process been handled differently, we may have had better tools to combat infringement abroad. As it stands, rights holders are often unable to take action against unscrupulous foreign actors who exploit their copyrights without permission.

SOPA's Senate companion, PROTECT-IP, was introduced before the House bill and was drafted in a more open process. I know because I brought actual artist stakeholders as well as Internet security and other technical experts to meet with Senate lawmakers and staff. PROTECT-IP was less flawed than SOPA but contained a few areas of concern, particularly a "private right of action" whereby copyright owners could compel a website to be blocked without any oversight or recourse. It's not hard to see a provision like this being used to thwart competition or, worse, as a green light to filter the Internet for political reasons. Debates about what does or doesn't constitute legitimate speech online are beyond this book's purview, but it is easy enough to recognize the slippery slope of giving private companies or nation-states the power to censor speech without due process.

SOPA also contained vague provisions with potential impacts that went well beyond its intended purpose. The legislation was endorsed by groups including the American Federation of Musicians, the American Association of Independent Music (A2IM), the RIAA, the Motion Picture Association of America, Songwriters Guild of America, the American Federation of Television and Radio Artists, the National Music Publishers Association (NMPA), and others. Some of these entities work to protect and advance the rights of creators. Others are more concerned with global market share, stock dividends, and quarterly profits. As one industry figure told me, any flaws in the legislation "could be fixed later." But that's not how these things tend to work—once a bill is enacted, it's very difficult to change. Just ask those rights holders who believe the Digital Millennium Copyright Act is flawed.

Opposing SOPA was a long list of public interest and consumer organizations, along with a number of technology companies and trade groups such as Google and the Consumer Electronics Association. It's true that some technology providers are known for taking aggressive stances against the entertainment sector. But here they made some good points: if enforcement rules are too restrictive, the next great innovation may never reach the marketplace, thereby depriving artists and other content creators of useful tools to distribute and promote their work.

Definitions Matter

SOPA's language around "infringing" sites and services were broad enough to include those with legitimate purposes. This seemed to contradict a key Supreme Court case from 1984, *Sony Corp. of America v. Universal City Studios, Inc.*, which held that a manufacturer of a product is not liable for infringement so long as the product is "capable of substantial noninfringing uses."[14] These days, a great many musicians and producers use tools like Dropbox to send files back and forth to collaborators. Under SOPA, similar services—and those yet to be invented—could have been subject to blocking or other penalties. Unlike the Senate bill with its more tailored definitions, SOPA would have allowed the targeting of any foreign site or service that "facilitates" infringement, based solely on a rights holder making the assertion.

Another issue with SOPA was how it treated a fundamental feature of the Internet—the domain name server (DNS) system. A kind of phonebook for the World Wide Web, DNS converts a site's numerical address to more easily remembered words and letters, like ledzeppelin.com. If a site appeared on a SOPA blacklist, it would no longer be "resolved" by the DNS system. However, it is a simple matter for a site to change domain names while keeping the same content. Furthermore, a user could also simply type in the numerical IP address and access the site without issue. SOPA's authors seemed to recognize how easy it is to get around DNS redirects, so they also authorized the U.S. attorney general to target any product or service fitting the statutory description. Recent history shows how this can be a problem. In 2011, the Immigrations and Customs Enforcement (ICE) division of the Department of Homeland Security took down the popular hip-hop blog Dajaz1.com based on false allegations of infringement.[15] It took a year to return property that ICE itself admitted was improperly seized. As it turned out, a major label's promotions team had been providing MP3s directly to the taste-making site. So who ordered the takedown? The RIAA, who apparently didn't even need SOPA to remove an entire website.

There are alternative mechanisms that could provide rights holders with relief without risks to legitimate expression. A follow-the-money approach (with due process provisions) would prevent the Internet's true bad actors from profiting off of American intellectual property. That's how U.S. law enforcement dealt with a proliferation of offshore gambling sites in the early days of broadband. Yet this proven approach was unfortunately not one of SOPA's remedies, nor has there been subsequent legislation to tackle the problem of international infringement in this way.

Takeaways from the SOPA Debate

In January 2012, the House of Representatives pulled its version of the bill due to a wave of public criticism. Shortly thereafter, the White House said it could not support bills that could censor legitimate online activity, inhibit innovation, or create new cybersecurity risks—all of which were the main concerns of the anti-SOPA community. The White House also stated that DNS provisions, a tentpole of both SOPA and PIPA, "pose a real risk to cybersecurity and yet leave contraband goods and services accessible online."[16] Which is what opponents of the legislation were saying all along. The administration suggested that any bills be "narrowly targeted only at sites beyond the reach of current US law"[17] and "prevent[ing] overly broad private rights of action."[18]

Among those voicing concerns about the scope of SOPA were copyright owners, creators, and curators, including thousands of members of arts and culture organizations as well as individual artists like MGMT, Trent Reznor, OK Go, Amanda Palmer, Jason Mraz, Zoë Keating, and more. "The battle over piracy doesn't really include artists," Keating said in 2012.[19] To me, this is the biggest problem with legislative proposals to combat online infringement. The only way to achieve sound policy in this area is through consultation with working artists and songwriters whose experiences may differ from large music and technology interests. Protecting intellectual property is crucial to a functioning economy, but so is understanding the experience of actual creators who provide the source material for copyright markets.

During the SOPA and PIPA debates, I was in regular contact with leaders in the music sector. I recall telling the then president of the independent label trade group, the A2IM that it made more sense to update the Digital Millennium Copyright Act (DMCA) than to filter the Internet at the DNS level. My suggestion fell on deaf ears, perhaps because so many powerful figures in the rights holder community backed SOPA. Turns out, all I had to do was wait a decade: current copyright enforcement proposals supported by the music industry put the DMCA front and center.

Recent Developments in Online Copyright Enforcement

As this book was going to press, there were a couple of significant legislative developments around copyright enforcement. The first is the establishment of a copyright small claims court via the Copyright Alternative in Small Claims Enforcement Act (CASE Act). This new law "creates a small-claims tribunal at the U.S. Copyright Office to make it easier and less expensive to lodge copyright disputes"[20] and gives rights holders who may not have the resources to bring court action a way to assert their rights as authors and owners of expressive works (including music). Critics have suggested that the new law could lead to an increase in "copyright trolls," but I think it's important that all authors—and not just the well heeled and well represented—are able to avail themselves of bedrock constitutional protections. Another bill that passed in late 2020 as part of pandemic relief legislation is the Protect Lawful Streaming Act. It harmonizes the penalties for illegal streaming with those for illegal downloading. This new law isn't aimed at users but rather the providers of illegal streams, making it a felony to engage in large-scale streaming of copyright material.

THE GREAT DMCA DEBATE

The DMCA is a hefty slab of federal legislation that became law in 1998. Section 512 of the DMCA sets the rules around "safe harbors." This is what allows search engines, user-upload sites, and social media platforms to function as we know them today. Under Section 512, online sites and services are obligated to remove or disable access to infringing material or links when notified by rights holders. This process is commonly referred to as "notice and takedown." A growing number of rights holders want to replace these rules with what they call "notice and *staydown*." Copyright owners describe a "whack-a-mole" problem whereby a removed track or video is reuploaded under many different links, each requiring a separate takedown notice. Proposed amendments to the DMCA would require digital service providers (DSPs) to take more aggressive action around repeat infringements, but rights holders are vague on specifics. DSPs strongly oppose expanding their obligations under the DMCA and accuse rights holders of abusing their position by sending takedown notices for content they don't control or for which there are exceptions to infringement. These debates touch on everything from free speech to the right of creators to derive economic benefit from their works. Which is why it's worth taking a deeper look at Section 512 of the DMCA as we consider the future of online copyright enforcement.

The Ins and Outs of Internet Safe Harbors

As previously described, safe harbors shield websites and other digital services from certain liabilities, provided the DSP takes steps to block or remove an alleged infringement upon receiving a properly composed takedown notice. It is important to note that safe harbors do not apply when a site or service encourages or ignores infringement. Section 512(c) of the DMCA denies eligibility to DSPs if there is "actual knowledge that the material or an activity using the material on the system or network is infringing."[21] Immunity is also unavailable to a site if it is "aware of facts or circumstances from which infringing activity is apparent."[22] If this seems confusing, take solace in the fact that courts have also had difficulty parsing the difference between "actual" and "red flag knowledge" as outlined in statute. The general idea is that in order to qualify for safe harbor, a site or service operator must not know about specific instances of infringement—either subjectively (actual knowledge) or objectively (red flag knowledge). Key judicial rulings have followed a less stringent application of these standards,[23] to the chagrin of some in the copyright community. All of which goes to show that even the most well-intended legislation can result in dissatisfaction among stakeholders due to variances in court interpretation.

A more clear-cut prohibition is when a site or service "induces" copyright infringement. Safe harbors are unavailable if executives or employees upload unauthorized content themselves or provide access to content they know is infringing (known as "vicarious liability"). In 2015, the streaming service Grooveshark—which once boasted more than 35 million users—was shuttered due to some combination of these activities.[24] The court's decision, like others before it, provides a bright-line legal standard that has reduced the number of unlicensed P2P platforms on the Internet. Nevertheless, DMCA safe harbor provisions remain controversial, especially among rights holders. Before we get to the reasons why, let's look at how safe harbor laws helped drive the growth of the Internet as we know it today.

Benefits of Safe Harbors

Though devised in the days of dial-up, online safe harbors make today's "social web" possible. The Internet provides for the dissemination of all kinds of expression, from personal opinion to popular music, making it hard to imagine a world without DMCA Section 512. There would certainly be no YouTube, Facebook, or Twitter, to say nothing of Google's ubiquitous search engine. Perhaps you think the aforementioned companies have too much control over our digital lives, a legitimate criticism that is beyond the scope of this book. But consider, too, services like Tunecore, CD Baby, Mailchimp, and Squarespace—all useful to musicians and all beneficiaries of safe harbors.

No matter how you look at it, the rules limiting liability for DSPs led to an explosion of innovative services that in turn drove consumer adoption of the Internet. By now, most music creators and rights holders have adapted to doing business online. In fact, artists are often early adopters. From MySpace to TikTok, musicians have helped drive the evolution of social media. Some artists, like Justin Bieber, launched their careers by posting videos to YouTube; there are now countless creators who use the site as a primary distribution platform. The opportunity to reach untold millions is likewise hard to resist for labels and publishers, even those who take aggressive positions on copyright infringement. In 2016, the notoriously litigious NMPA reached an agreement with YouTube whereby its members' repertoire would be directly licensed to the service. Like their record label counterparts, publishers were drawn to the negotiating table by YouTube's massive userbase and advertising revenue.[25] Despite these and other deals, however, rights holders remain mistrustful of YouTube and its parent company Google, who they see as unfairly benefitting from Internet safe harbors.

DMCA Pain Points

There are some who believe there should be no online safe harbors at all. That would be a real buzzkill for millions of everyday Internet users. Share a meme that includes a copyrighted image? You just infringed. Play Britney Spears in a livestreamed '90s dance party? Oops, you did it again. Prior lawsuits against illegal downloaders prove that anyone can be sued, even grandma.[26] With statutory damages up to $150,000 per work for "willful infringement" (where the unsanctioned activity is intentional), penalties for copyright violations can be steep indeed. Based on recent litigation, DSPs would be the most likely targets if safe harbors disappeared. But just about everyone would be affected if user-upload and social media services faced strict liability for copyright infringement. Some sites might simply fold. As someone who has deleted their Twitter more than once, the thought does have some appeal. However, this would be a net negative for creativity and commerce, to say nothing of cat memes. The good news is that such hardline views are unlikely to find favor with policymakers. But that doesn't mean the law will remain exactly as it is today.

Current efforts to modify the DMCA focus on the specific rules governing notice and takedown. There is international precedent for safe harbor reform; in 2019, the Directive on Copyright in the Digital Single Market (Article 17) became law in Europe. The directive contains provisions compelling DSPs that host user-uploaded content to adopt "effective and proportionate" measures to protect copyright. With more than three hundred hours of video and audio uploaded to YouTube daily, it is impossible for human beings to assess the copyright status of so much material. This means DSPs will use automated detection technology to identify and block uploads of copyrighted content. There are well-founded concerns, however, about such systems being used to quash legitimate expression.

Watching the Detection

Today, most user-upload sites employ some form of copyright detection. DSPs tend to use technologies from third-party providers or build proprietary systems (such as YouTube's Content ID). The big labels and Hollywood studios also employ automation to issue takedown notices. Yet smaller companies and individual creators may not be in a position to implement tracking software or pay others to scour the web on their behalf. Which is why rights holders want to shift the burden of enforcement to DSPs. An updated DMCA would likely include a mandate for services to have a system to identify copyrighted works.[27] However, such a mandate could increase costs for technology start-ups, who, like smaller labels and publishers, may not have the resources to devote to detection. Which is why it would be a good idea for lawmakers to study the current marketplace for copyright identification to determine the feasibility of a federal requirement. Also helpful would be a technical standards body comprising private market participants who could produce guidelines for implementation. Of course, identifying copyrighted content is much easier when rights holders enumerate what music they control. This is why proper music metadata and accessible databases containing information on ownership are crucial to the digital music ecosystem. (More on that in the following chapter.)

The "Value Gap"

Labels and publishers have accused YouTube of using its safe harbors to pay below-market rates for licensing music content because there's always the notice-and-takedown system to fall back on. You may have heard this referred to as the "value gap." According to the RIAA, interactive services like Spotify pay seven times more per stream than YouTube.[28] This is true even though nine out of the top ten most watched videos on YouTube are music videos, and some 82 percent of all YouTube visitors go there for music.[29] Labels and publishers complain that YouTube pushes for lower licensing fees in take-it-or-leave-it deals where walking away means having to spend time and money sending takedown notices for every infringement. Those who accept YouTube's rates are allowed into its Content ID system; in the view of some music companies, this is no better than a protection racket.

Content ID has also been criticized for the accuracy of its detection algorithms. YouTube counters these allegations by pointing out that it built this system at its own expense and that any issues with audio matching stem from the poor-quality metadata provided by rights holders. Even where the system works as intended, there can be grievances. For example, some rights holders are upset that YouTube doesn't return money made from placing ads around infringing content *before* a link is disabled. Services argue that rights holders often issue takedowns for content that they don't control (or only partially control), depriving YouTube content creators of opportunities to earn revenue, to say nothing of their own expressive rights.

Often these issues are reduced to talking points or are exaggerated beyond credulity. This can make it harder to find common ground, which is key to achieving policies that balance the interests of all parties: content creators, copyright owners, and everyday Internet users. In the case of DMCA Section 512, consensus—which typically includes compromise—might involve standardized technical measures that copyright owners and services can use to detect, deter, and disable infringement, along with a dispute resolution process whereby counterclaims can be resolved. Algorithms could begin to "learn" what is and isn't a legitimate takedown, which would create more confidence around automated blocking—the "staydown" so many rights holders want implemented. Is compromise along these lines possible? The passage of the Music Modernization Act in 2018 shows that it's possible for stakeholders to find common ground on persistent problems. Of course, just because they *can* doesn't mean they will. Currently, it seems that the loudest voices in the safe harbors debate are reluctant to form a chorus.

WHO'S THE FAIREST OF THEM ALL?

Chances are you've come across music posted to YouTube where the uploader wrote "no infringement intended" in the text description. To be crystal clear: These invocations are no protection against copyright strikes. Worse, they can perpetuate misunderstanding about what is and isn't allowable on user-upload services under federal law. It's also common to see references to "fair use" in such disclaimers. While it's true that fair use contains important exceptions to copyright liability, it is by no means a green light to infringe. With so much confusion around these issues, it's good to take a closer look at fair use to better understand how and where it applies.

At its most simple, fair use allows someone to use copyrighted works without permission under certain conditions. Section 107 of the Copyright Act establishes the framework for fair use. The statutory language specifies as key criteria criticism, commentary, reporting, education, and research. Fair use exceptions can extend to parody and "transformative" uses, but this isn't a hard-and-fast rule—determinations of fairness are highly context dependent. A use may qualify as fair in one context while it would be considered infringing in another. In order for a use to be deemed fair, someone needs to sue for infringement, and that someone needs to invoke fair use as a so-called affirmative defense. A judge then looks at the evidence specific to the case and balances the four factors in Section 107 to arrive at a decision. Depending on the evidence, these factors can be weighted differently—not all determinations of fairness satisfy all four criteria.

Let's take a closer look at the four-factor fair use test:

1. The purpose and type (or "character") of the use, including whether such use is of a commercial nature or is for nonprofit educational purposes.

    Some uses are more likely to be considered fair if the activity is noncommercial or educational in nature—exceptions that allow for constructive dialog around existing works through excerpts and references. The first factor can also include "transformative uses" where the activity produces something new, as opposed to a straight copy of the original. People sometimes think this automatically applies to sampling and remixes, but the issue is not so clear-cut.

    Determining what is or isn't transformative can be a challenge. It often comes down to the degree of transformation (the more transformed, the more likely a use is fair). Parody provides a good example. Technically, parodies are supposed to comment upon the original work, which means satire isn't automatically covered. Even "Weird Al" Yankovic errs on the safe side and always asks permission from the performers and songwriters of the music he parodies. The Supreme Court has acknowledged parody as a possible exception but reiterated that it's not an automatic guarantor of fairness.[30] As I said, much depends on the overall circumstances of a use (and even a judge's own understanding of the law).

    Educational uses might seem more obviously fair, but it can still be tricky. Consider the popular YouTuber Rick Beato. A musician, songwriter, and recording engineer, Beato built a considerable following with his instructional videos and analysis of classic rock music. He has also been on the receiving end of copyright takedowns for videos that have garnered millions of views. One of Beato's videos that was removed examines the history of rock guitar and features a mere ten seconds of an improvised solo by Ozzy Osbourne's late guitarist Randy Rhoads.[31] Other online music instructors have had their videos blocked over a single chord.[32] If an uploader doesn't understand their rights, such copyright strikes may go unchallenged, thereby depriving the public of potentially useful information. These and other examples also reveal the limitations of automated takedowns. If a judge has difficulty determining whether a use is fair, it's a good bet that an algorithm isn't up to the challenge.

2. The nature of the copyrighted work.

This factor is pretty straightforward but may be weighted differently from case to case alongside the other factors. In general, there is greater leeway for using "factual works" such as news items, technical manuals, or biographies than there is for fictional works like novels, movies, plays, or songs. A fair use claim that includes this factor is likely to be more successful if the work copied has already been published. The reason is that the original author has the exclusive right over how their expression is first made publicly available.

3. The amount and substantiality of the portion used in relation to the copyrighted work as a whole.

When weighing this factor, judges consider the quantity and quality of the work that was used. If the use includes a large portion of the copyrighted work, fair use is less likely to be found; if the use employs only a small amount of copyrighted material, fair use is more likely. That said, some courts have found use of an entire work to be fair under certain circumstances. And yet in other cases, the use of even small amounts of a work was deemed infringing because the portion used was considered the "heart" of the original. Given these nuances, you can see why some people think they're immune to infringement claims because they only used a tiny amount of a work. But much like the "five second rule" for food dropped on the floor, this is mostly a myth.

Actually, there are some allowances for *de minimis* uses of underlying compositions (where the amount is deemed too trivial to merit consideration). A 2003 case involved the Beastie Boys's sample of three notes of a composition originally performed on flute, for which they had already licensed the sound recording. Although fair use was *not* invoked as a defense, the court nevertheless found no infringement due to the small amount used.[33] The situation is different for sound recordings, however. *Bridgeport Music, Inc. v. Dimension Films* involved a two-second guitar loop, lowered in pitch, that hip-hop group N.W.A. sampled for their track "100 Miles and Runnin," which appeared on the soundtrack of the movie *I Got the Hook Up*. The owner of the Funkadelic track that was sampled, Bridgeport Music Inc., filed suit. A federal judge found no copyright violation, but the U.S. Court of Appeals for the Sixth Circuit reversed the ruling in 2005. "Get a license or do not sample," the opinion admonished. This decision essentially tosses out the *de minimis* doctrine as applied to sound recordings (at least in the Sixth Circuit) and has impacted industry practices around sampling.

Interestingly, the *Bridgeport* decision did not preclude other defenses such as fair use. But because the defendants didn't argue based on fair use, no precedent was established.[34] One prominent sampling artist, Gregg Gillis, who produces mashups under the name Girl Talk, believes his work qualifies as fair use (more on the basis of transformation than amount). Yet sound recording owners seem reluctant to challenge this belief in court. Why? Because if a fair use defense is successful, it would set precedent for sound recordings that could impact the market for sample licensing. Fees for audio samples, however small, tend to be whatever the market can bear. Depending on various factors, sample clearance for sound recordings can run from a couple grand to $10,000. This is probably cheaper than damages from a lawsuit, so for now, it's best to follow the judge's advice in *Bridgeport* and get permission for both the underlying composition *and* the sound recording if you intend to sample music in a new work.

4. The effect of the use upon the potential market for or value of the copyrighted work.

This factor is about whether a use deprives the copyright owner of income or otherwise undermines the market (or potential market) for an existing work. In its explainer on fair use, the U.S. Copyright Office says that "courts consider whether the use is hurting the current market for the original work (for example, by displacing sales of the original) and/or whether the use could cause substantial harm if it were to become widespread."[35] This factor often works in tandem with the "purpose" of a use. Market impacts are harder to prove in instances of research or scholarship; an adverse effect is more easily established for commercial uses. Still, it's difficult to predict how this factor will be applied, and rulings have been all over the map. I have been surprised to see lawsuits brought for uses that seem unlikely to affect the market for a work and are also unlikely to displace sales. Let's take a look at one of them now.

Case Study: *Lenz v. Universal Music*

A somewhat recent court case, *Lenz v. Universal Music*, illustrates the tensions between fair use and notice and takedown. Back in 2007, a mother named Stephanie Lenz made a video of her young children dancing in her kitchen. In the background, "Let's Go Crazy" by Prince "can be heard for approximately twenty seconds, albeit with . . . poor sound quality."[36] And by poor quality, I mean barely audible; most people would struggle to imagine the snippet impacting the market for the actual track. At the behest of the copyright owner, YouTube removed the video, which prompted Lenz to send a DMCA counter-notification. The video was restored, but the case continued.

The DMCA requires copyright owners to have a "good faith belief" that an upload is actually infringing or else they may be in violation of the law. In practice, a copyright owner doesn't have to do much at all to back up a copyright claim, which some—including groups like the Electronic Frontier Foundation and Lenz herself—say creates the conditions for abuse. Shortly after YouTube restored her video, Lenz sued Universal for failing to comply with the good faith requirement. This was a provocative move, especially considering that copyright lawsuits tend to be brought by rights holders and not every day Internet users. The Northern District of California found that the party issuing a takedown "must evaluate whether the material makes fair use of the copyright"[37] but let Universal off the hook with its opinion that the good faith standard is subjective rather than objective. Which is to say, the burden was on Lenz to "demonstrate that Universal had some actual knowledge that its Takedown Notice contained a material misrepresentation."[38] In 2013, the District Court rejected parties' request for summary judgment (a ruling without full trial), setting the stage for both Lenz and Universal to appeal.

In a 2015 ruling, the U.S. Court of Appeals for the Ninth Circuit affirmed the earlier decision but appeared to set new precedent around fair use and takedowns. In its decision, the court unambiguously situated fair use within the DMCA's good faith requirement, stating that rights holders have a "duty to consider—in good faith and prior to sending a takedown notification—whether allegedly infringing material constitutes fair use."[39] At first blush, this decision appears to place rights holders under a potentially burdensome requirement to consider whether user-uploaded material containing some portion of a work they control is fair. But that's not exactly what the court is saying here. By upholding the previous ruling that the good faith requirement is subjective, the Ninth Circuit gives rights holders a great deal of leeway. Remember, copyright owners don't have to be correct in their failing to recognize an actual fair use. Further, in order for a rights holder to be held liable for violating its obligations under the DMCA, a plaintiff would have to prove they acted in bad faith. That's a hard thing to demonstrate as it essentially requires evidence of someone's frame of mind. The lack of precedental guidelines for what is or isn't fair use in music may encourage rights holders to remain ignorant of this part of copyright law if it helps maintain their belief that a takedown notice was appropriately crafted. The mass automation of this process, aided by detection technologies, adds a new wrinkle. Machines don't have mindsets to evaluate. Not at this time, anyway.

The *Lenz* is fascinating because it touches on several different aspects of the copyright enforcement debates. First there is federal statute, which establishes the rules for the dissemination of expressive works and defines the exclusive rights conferred on authors and owners of copyright (as well as exceptions to those exclusivities). Then there are the courts, which rely on prior precedent as well as statutory interpretation in the consideration of evidence specific to a copyright case. Last, there is user behavior and corporate business practices being brought into conflict by technological innovation. A recent example involves Metallica, who as you recall were front and center in the original debates about P2P. In early 2021, the band was booked to kick off Blizzcon, an event promoting the video game company Blizzard, livestreamed on the

COPYRIGHT ENFORCEMENT, SAFE HARBORS, AND FAIR USE 87

popular gaming site Twitch. Unfortunately, the mighty Metallica found their muscular rock replaced by piddling production music due to the site's concerns over infringement. It just goes to show that technology and evolving modes of consumption will continue to test the limits of the law, occasionally with karmically amusing results.

These tensions are unlikely to be resolved until Congress decides to update or replace existing laws. Over the past decade, there has been an uptick in enthusiasm for a comprehensive overhaul of the Copyright Act, but an approach for doing so remains elusive. Whether this is by happenstance or design is beyond my reckoning. I do know that finding solutions that work for a universe of stakeholders are even more challenging in an increasingly partisan Washington. At some point, however, courts' ability to arrive at cogent decisions will be compromised by outdated statute. Some would say that point has already passed. If so, it is even more urgent to reestablish a framework for copyright that protects the rights of authors and preserves their incentive to create while allowing for works to be disseminated, enjoyed, and, where appropriate, made constructive use of in new forms of expression.

7

COPYRIGHT REGISTRATION, METADATA, AND DATABASES

In this chapter, we will look at a few interconnected topics:

- Copyright Registration: how to register works with the U.S. Copyright Office
- Music Metadata: information relevant to a work, its author(s) and owners
- Ownership Databases: storehouses of information about copyright ownership, creator splits, and permitted uses

I'll describe the process for registering music copyrights, bust a few myths, and offer insight on how to protect your own works. I'll also fill you in on the debates about music metadata and databases—a hot-button issue that's only gotten hotter. Rights holders and services have had much difficulty identifying tracks and matching usage across a mind-boggling array of global digital distribution platforms. Transparency, accuracy, and efficiency are crucial to ensuring that proper parties are paid when music is commercially exploited, or else we risk perpetuating the inequities of the earlier industry or, worse, creating new ones.

Last, you'll learn about efforts to achieve better systems for rights management and royalties and why it's taken so long to get there. We'll also consider some of the technical aspects of managing the global music "dataflood," including the much ballyhooed blockchain—a new technology that promises to revolutionize how music is tracked and monetized. But don't worry, a degree in computer science isn't necessary to follow along, which is good, because I don't have one.

All of these issues are important to recognize as the music business continues its transition to a largely digital distribution model. Let's kick our investigations off with a look at registration with the U.S. Copyright Office (USCO), which is important for individual creators as well as those who manage music repertoires.

COPYRIGHT FORMALITIES

For much of the history of copyright in America—102 years to be exact—registration with the Copyright Office was a requirement for works to be recognized and published. This changed when Congress passed the Berne Convention Implementation Act of 1988, which did away with so-called formalities, conferring copyright status the moment an original expression is "fixed in a tangible medium."[1] This legislation brought America into partial compliance with the Berne Convention for the Protection of Literary and Artistic Works (typically known as the Berne Convention)—an international agreement concerning copyright, which was originally established in Berne, Switzerland, back in 1886. I say "partial compliance" because the Berne Convention also provides for something called moral rights, which the United States has thus far chosen not to adopt. Moral rights give creators the right to attribution and allow them to object to uses that affect the integrity of the work or that are "prejudicial to the author's honor or reputation."[2] Some have called for the United States to recognize such rights, but there has been no meaningful legislative movement to date.

Although copyright is automatic, it is highly recommended to register works with the Copyright Office in order to assert your rights or seek damages for infringement. Registration provides a public record of your claim to a work and establishes *prima facie* (at first sight) evidence of ownership, which can aid in the resolution of disputes. Think of copyright registration as a fairly inexpensive, but nonetheless important, form of insurance. We'll get into the fees and process for registration shortly; first let's look at the role the Copyright Office plays in maintaining the national record of expressive works and their authors/owners.

The U.S. Copyright Office

In 1870, the Library of Congress (LOC) was tasked with managing copyright registrations; previously, this had been handled by district court clerks. In 1897, the U.S. Copyright Office was established as a department of the LOC, taking on the role of recordation (figure 7.1). Appointed by the Librarian of Congress, the Register of Copyrights is responsible for the overall functioning of the office, its departments, and its staff. With more than six hundred thousand copyright applications processed per year, there's plenty to oversee. In addition to processing copyright applications and maintaining records, the USCO also plays an important role in how copyright law is interpreted and enforced. Here are some of its core activities:

Figure 7.1. The U.S. Copyright Office, Washington, DC.

- Advises Congress on the status of domestic and international copyright issues
- Analyzes and helps formulate copyright legislation
- Conducts studies to aid in legislative decision making around copyright
- Assists developing nations in establishing their own copyright laws
- Issues regulations around key provisions in the Copyright Act and publishes these regulations in the Federal Register
- Helps educate the public about copyright law and departmental practices (the office does not offer legal advice in infringement lawsuits or other matters)
- Publishes informational circulars and website posts summarizing various copyright issues

Before I lived and worked in Washington, DC, I imagined the USCO to be a subterranean vault with miles of aisles, sort of like where they stash the Ark of the Covenant at the end of the first Indiana Jones movie. This isn't the case, although the aforementioned movie is among the registered works housed there. In actuality, the Copyright Office is a boxy but not inelegant building on 101 Independence Avenue, S.E., in Washington, DC, open to the public from 8:30 a.m. to 5:00 p.m. on weekdays. (Having had a private tour, I can confirm that there's some neat stuff in the basement, but I never saw the Ark.) If you're not local, there's plenty to peruse at www.copyright.gov, where you can find useful information on various proceedings, events, analyses, and information on how to register your copyrights. Even better, you can register copyrights online and deposit electronic copies of works.

Copyright Office Divisions for Registration

The functions of the USCO are carried out by various departments; at the moment, we're concerned with three: the Receipt Analysis and Control Division, the Registration Program, and the Information and Records Division. These departments cover most of the activities relevant to registration and search:

1. Receipt Analysis and Control Division

    This department receives and processes registration applications and fees. It also maintains all correspondence relevant to registration and resolves incomplete claims. The division assigns registration numbers and certifies registration via mailed certificates to filants.

2. Registration Program

    This department contains three subgroups: the Literary, Performing Arts, and Visual Arts divisions review registration and renewal applications pertaining to each field. The Registration Program also examines deposit copies of works alongside the required forms to ensure the information is correct and that the works satisfy the criteria for copyright. Note that the USCO only registers *claims* of copyright authorship or ownership; it doesn't weigh in on the validity of such claims. If registration forms are incomplete, a Registration Program examiner will contact the applicant to resolve any issues.

3. Information and Records Division

    This department produces and distributes informational materials relevant to copyright records for both the public and USCO staff. For an hourly fee, it also can prepare search reports upon request. Such reports can contain information about specific works, their claimants, and how ownership was secured. In the instance of copyright transfers from one owner to another, the Information and Records Division certifies and facilitates recordation of pertinent documents relating to the transfer.

Why Register?

Copyright registration is simply a claim of ownership to a work as of a specific date. As I previously mentioned, registration is optional. By doing so, however, you assert the right to protect your interests over works you authored and own. As stated in Section 408(a) of the Copyright Act,

> The owner of copyright or of any exclusive right in the work may obtain registration of the copyright claim by delivering to the Copyright Office

the deposit specified by this section, together with the application and fee specified by sections 409 and 708. Such registration is not a condition of copyright protection.

Registration also gives the copyright owner the ability to sue for infringement. Section 411(a) of the Copyright Act requires registration as a precondition for filing suit. This applies only to works first published in the United States (or simultaneously in America and another territory). If a work is first published in another country and the owner is not a U.S. citizen or resident, this does not apply. It's best to register early in order to give time for processing, which can take up to six months. As previously noted, early registration gives the copyright owner the ability to collect attorney fees and statutory damages. Provided an infringement claim is successful, an owner is eligible for these benefits if a work is registered *before* a copyright violation occurs (or three months after its initial publication). Expedited registration is available; at the time of this writing, the Copyright Office fee for "special handling" is $800 per work. (This is subject to change, so be sure to check the USCO website for current rates.)

Again, the USCO doesn't make determinations about the validity of a claim but merely records it. Sometimes this results in disputes. Let's say someone registers a copyright and claims ownership, but in reality the work belongs to another party. If you, as owner of the work, were able to present sufficient proof for a court to validate your claim, the court would toss the phony registration, at which point you could file a proper application with the USCO. Or perhaps you are the rightful owner and your work is used without permission. Registration can be beneficial even if your case doesn't go to trial as many infringement claims end up being settled between parties. If a work is registered, infringers may pursue settlement to avoid high statutory damages and paying the plaintiff's legal fees.

Registering Joint Works

In chapter 4, I described the complexities of musical works, which can involve multiple authors and owners. The process for registering with the USCO is open to anyone who owns part or all of the exclusive rights that attach to a copyrightable work. For musical compositions, this includes any of the songwriters, as well as parties acquiring ownership of one or more exclusivities. That sounds complicated, but the good news is that just one registration is sufficient to protect all owners. However, the proper payment of royalties for the exploitation of any exclusivity requires information on splits and associated fees, which is not the role of the Copyright Office. This is why quality metadata and accessible databases are essential to the collection and distribution of royalties, which we will examine later in this chapter.

Typically, if a songwriter transfers ownership of a song to a publisher, the publisher would be the one to register the song with the USCO. The same is true for a recording artist and their label. If you're a signed songwriter or a recording artist (or both), it's good to make sure this has actually happened. I personally know a songwriter whose publisher failed to register one of her compositions, which was later infringed. Suffice it to say, this created difficulties in seeking an injunction to stop the offending use and did not result in a settlement or damage award.

When to Register and How Much Does It Cost?

You can register a work at any time in the life of the copyright (which as you recall is life plus seventy years or, for works of corporate authorship, ninety-five years from first publication or 120 years from creation, whichever expires first). However, it's better to register earlier, preferably within three months of the work's initial publication, as this is what lets you collect damages and attorney's fees. The smartest approach is to register as soon as you're ready to publish a work (or have set a date for publication).

Some copyright owners and authors may drag their feet on registering their copyrights due to the application fees, which can add up if you're registering multiple works. These fees are nonrefundable, which means you don't get that money back if your work fails to generate revenue. Registration fees depend on the type of work being registered and the filing method. The Copyright Office recommends electronic filing for most applications; this also happens to be the cheaper option. The standard filing fee for electronic registration is $65 for basic claims. However, the filing fee is $45 if you register one work, not made for hire, and you are the only author and claimant. The fee for a basic registration using paper forms is $125 payable by check or money order.[3] Remember, successful applications require the proper filling out of associated forms, the payment of the application fee, and the depositing of a copy of the work.

Generally, copyright registration is per individual work, which requires a separate application, filing fee, and deposit for each. However, there are limited exceptions to this rule, which the Copyright Office describes as follows:

- When a number of separate and independent contributions are assembled into a collective whole (collective works)
- When multiple unpublished works, serials, newspapers, newsletters, contributions to periodicals, photographs, database updates, or secure test items meet Copyright Office requirements for registration on one application (group registrations)
- When multiple works are physically bundled or packaged together and first published as an integrated unit (unit of publication)
- When the copyright claimant for a sound recording and the musical, literary, or dramatic work embodied in the recording is the same individual or organization[4]

How to Register

All of the information you need to register your copyrights is available at the USCO website, but I'll also describe the process here. It's not terribly difficult to apply, but you'll want to have your ducks in a row before doing so. There are two ways to apply for copyright registration:

1. Fill out an application with the Electronic Copyright Office (eCO) at the USCO website.
2. Submit a paper application form to the Copyright Office via regular U.S. mail.

You don't need to say an incantation or light a candle; just make sure the information on the forms is correct and that you've also submitted a copy of the work (deposit) and paid the appropriate application fee.

COPYRIGHT REGISTRATION, METADATA, AND DATABASES 97

The USCO recommends online registration as the fastest and cheapest way of submitting an application. The vast majority of applications are now processed this way since the eCO system was launched back in 2008. Despite the efficiencies of online submissions, it can still take up to three months to process. But compare that to eleven months for paper applications, and you can see the clear incentive for e-filing. As previously mentioned, the fee is less for eCO filings as well: $45 vs. $125 for basic claims. Here are the specific steps for filing a copyright application online:

- Head to copyright.gov and click on the Register tab.
- Click on the eCO link.
- Create an account with eCO to obtain a user ID and password. Hang on to those as you'll need them to access your application.
- Follow the prompts to complete the application.
- Review all of your carefully entered information and then click "Checkout."
- Pay the application fee, which is required before you upload your deposit (a digital copy of the work).
- Upload your deposit by attaching it to your online application. If you don't have a digital copy of your work or it doesn't meet the criteria for uploading, you can request a shipping label to send by mail.
- When all of these steps are completed, the eCO will verify your submission and provide a case number for each application. You'll also get an email confirmation to the address you provided at the outset. Hang on to that in case you need to get in touch with the USCO regarding your claim.

Pretty straightforward, all things considered. The USCO also has helpful guides for different types of works; music falls under the Performing Arts category. As of 2019, you can submit no more than ten works under the Group of Unpublished Works designation. Works submitted as a group must have the same authors and coauthors with the title of each work listed. If you have only ten songs on an album, you could submit them under this category by selecting "Sound Recording." You can do the same to register a group of musical works that are embodied in each recording. But keep in mind that to register musical works in this way, the songwriter and recording artist need to be the same person or persons.

Chances are, you'll choose to register via eCO. But in case you're old school, here is the process for submitting paper applications using what is called Form CO:

- First, check the box to indicate what kind of work you are registering. Keep in mind that Form CO doesn't allow for group registrations.
- Form CO is on paper, but you'll still need to complete it online and then print it out. USCO will reject forms that are printed blank and then filled out or altered with ink after being completed online. Photocopies are not allowed. (You can see why eCO is preferable.)
- Print the form. A shipping label required for mailing the application and deposit will automatically print with Form CO.
- Mail the application, deposit, and application fee.

The Copyright Office also accepts traditional paper registration forms, which can be downloaded and filled out offline. The SR form should be used to register sound recordings; you can also use that same form to register the underlying compositions, but once again only if the owner is the same party and you specify that your application is meant to cover both sides of the musical copyright (sound recording and musical work). You can order forms via telephone by calling 202-707-9100; leave a message with your name, mailing address, and the type of form you require. If time is of no concern, you can also request forms by mail by writing to: Library of Congress Copyright Office-COPUBS, 101 Independence Avenue, S.E., Washington, DC, 20559. Or you could just do it the easy way and register online via eCO.

Preregistration Options

Although some choose to wait until a work is published to apply for copyright registration as a cost-saving measure, the Copyright Office also allows preregistration for certain works, including sound recordings and musical works. This policy was instituted as part of the 2005 Artists'

Rights and Theft Prevention Act, which recognized that certain media, like music and movies, are often "leaked" online before their release date. In order to be eligible for preregistration, a work must not yet be commercially available but in the process of readying for release. This applies primarily to corporate owners of copyright who have reason to believe a work or works are attractive to pirates to distribute widely. The online-only preregistration option costs $115 per work but does not require deposit.

The Review Process

Upon receiving your application, the USCO will examine the form(s) and deposit materials and issue a certificate of registration if everything is in order. Again, it's important to remember that the Copyright Office doesn't resolve disputes over claims, which are left to the courts to determine based on evidence. However, a valid copyright registration ranks high among the evidence a court would review, so filing with the USCO is a good insurance policy in the case of infringement.

Typically, the Copyright Office issues a response to claims within six months after receiving applications. Sometimes they can take longer; the COVID-19 pandemic would be a situation where one might expect delays. Should examiners find errors or omissions in your submission, it will be returned with a letter (or email) explaining the steps necessary to correct the application. Common reasons for rejection include:

- No signature on the application form
- Failure to pay the application fee
- Failure to deposit work(s)
- No description of the nature of the work and its authorship
- No specification of a transfer to a new claimant (change in ownership)
- Failure to describe new copyrightable material in a derivative work

All of this would be automatically flagged by the eCO system, which is another incentive to file electronically. Overall, it is rare for the Copyright Office to reject an application; under the so-called rule of doubt, USCO often grants copyright even where there is some question about the work's eligibility. In such an instance, applicants will often receive a letter stating that the work may not be valid but has nonetheless been registered. Should the claim be challenged, courts would consider this information in making a determination.

"Poor Man's Copyright" Debunked

You probably have heard about workarounds to registering with the Copyright Office. The most persistent of these concerns "poor man's copyright," whereby you put a copy of your work (say, a CD, cassette, or computer drive) in an envelope, seal it, and mail it to yourself without opening it. This allegedly serves as proof that the work was "fixed in a tangible medium" no later than the postmark. It's important to understand that this is not a foolproof alternative to USCO registration. Just because you mailed your work to yourself doesn't verify authorship or ownership as anyone could have put that CD, cassette, or drive into the envelope. Furthermore, even if this serves to indicate the work wasn't created after the postmark, you would not be eligible to receive statutory damages or attorney's fees should infringement occur. Therefore it's recommended that you file applications with the Copyright Office rather than take your chances on a sketchy substitute.

Copyright Notices

Once a work is copyrighted, you can demonstrate its protected status with three identifiers displayed together:

- The word "copyright" or the symbol © for musical works. For sound recordings, use the symbol for phonorecords: ℗.
- The year of initial publication (if unpublished, the year of fixation in a tangible medium).
- The name of the copyright owner. This may not be the author of the work, which is why when you click on an album or track on Spotify and scroll down, you typically see the label name along with these other two data points. On a physical copy of an album or single, you may also see the name of the publisher who controls the underlying composition(s) and sometimes the songwriters.[5]

Copyright notices often include the phrases "all rights reserved" or "unauthorized reproduction is prohibited by law." Last, if a third party has permission to distribute a work, you may see "under exclusive license to" or "used by permission" alongside the other designations. This information typically accompanies all reproductions of a work in a place it can be readily seen (album sleeve, landing page, printed sheet music, etc.). Unfortunately, it's also common for people who *haven't* registered with the USCO to use some combination of these notices. There's not much to be done about this as copyright is automatic for qualifying works, even if copyright *notices* are meant to be used by those whose claims have been granted by the Copyright Office.

Now that we've taken a somewhat comprehensive look at the Copyright Office and the registration/recordation process, it's time to consider how the marketplace deals with sound recordings and musical works for the purpose of collecting and distributing royalties and other fees. And that all comes down to music metadata and databases, which is part of a larger conversation about transparency in the music industry.

MUSIC DATA AND THE PURSUIT OF TRANSPARENCY

The Internet has opened up new avenues for artists to be heard around the world with the click of a mouse or the tap of a screen. It has also created challenges in the collection and distribution of royalties. Even in countries like the United States, where there is a well-established music business and a latticework of laws to govern it, there are frustrations with the mechanics of compensation. Much of this is the direct result of a lack of transparency in how music creators and rights holders are paid, how revenue shares are allocated, and what information is necessary to distribute royalties in a timely fashion. For their part, services struggle with a lack of accessible information on rights ownership, which increases liability and limits investment.

Transparency is a word that gets tossed around a lot in this business. At its most simple, it means that there is accessible and comprehensible information on licensing terms, revenue flows, and copyright ownership. A truly transparent music industry would mean that artists, composers, rights holders, and services would be operating with the same information sets within structures that allow for efficient and accurate royalties reporting. Obviously, there would still be debates about rate-setting fees and obligations, but what we're talking about here is the backbone data and infrastructure necessary to power a global digital music economy. The first and most essential unit of this infrastructure is music metadata.

WHAT IS MUSIC METADATA?

In the digital realm, metadata is the information that identifies and accompanies various kinds of files that can be read by and stored on computers. Music metadata may include text or numbers to identify the track, its authors, and its owners. When you play a song from your hard drive or a streaming service, you will most likely see the name of the song, the performing artist, and the album title. That's all metadata. Other information that fits this category are UPC and ISRC codes (more on these in a moment). These data travel with the music as it's distributed to various services, which aids in the discovery, attribution, and monetization of music files.

These days, digital music services have millions and millions of tracks available for purchase or to stream. With a massive amount of information to track and display, services face challenges in how they organize consumer-facing data, particularly on mobile apps. From iTunes to Spotify, there's been particular frustration about how classical music is presented on digital services. For example, Beethoven isn't the performer of his "9th Symphony," but if you're searching by title, chances are that's how it's displayed. Even if you know the name of the symphony orchestra, you could end up sifting through dozens, even hundreds, of tracks to find the recording you're looking for. Songwriters have also complained that they are not included in the display metadata on many commercial services. Spotify has taken some steps to rectify this with its "show credits" pop-up function as well as the recently launched Songwriters Hub, which gives users access to songwriter-centric playlists and podcasts. There is also a movement to surface information about producers and engineers, for whom attribution is helpful for getting gigs.

COPYRIGHT REGISTRATION, METADATA, AND DATABASES 103

Proper metadata is also crucial for matching to user consumption and delivering royalties to music creators. If certain information about a track is missing (like who owns a sound recording or underlying composition), it can cause problems when it's time to report and pay royalties to rights holders, PROs, and other royalty administrators. Where there are compulsory licenses, such "unattributed income" can end up in so-called black boxes. After a certain time (typically three years), the money in these black boxes is distributed to rights holders by market share. This means that major labels and publishers can and do get to keep revenue that should have gone to independent artists and songwriters.

Poor-quality metadata means that artists and songwriters may not get paid accurately, on time, or at all. Although major labels and publishers often enjoy free money from black boxes, problems with music metadata aren't necessarily a dark conspiracy. As a track makes its way from the studio to services, there are any number of entities in the supply chain responsible for some portion of information about a track. This can include parties who played a role in a song's creation or are responsible for monitoring usage and reporting to rights holders. Composers, songwriters, recording artists, background and session musicians, record labels, managers, publishers, producers, PROs, aggregators, distributors, services, and database operators all have some role to play in metadata hygiene. If key information isn't where it needs to be, it's unlikely to be passed along or filled in downstream.

I've heard poor-quality metadata described as "garbage in, garbage out." This means that any system to track ownership, authorship, distribution, and usage is only as good as the information contained within that system. This is useful to keep in mind when discussing new methods of data management, such as blockchain. Because it really doesn't matter what technology is used to house or exchange data if the data itself is insufficient. Metadata issues can arise in numerous contexts, which not only can deprive music creators of income but can also make it more difficult to resolve cross-claims between rights holders and create potential liability for services. Here is a partial list of metadata challenges that often arise in the realms of distribution, matching, and reporting:

- Source data: Who collects and organizes information about a song's creators and performers?
- Verification: How accurate is this data, and what is the mechanism for updating if necessary? This is a big issue with sound recordings that are often distributed without complete information on songwriters and songwriting splits. What if there are mistakes in the source metadata? Who is responsible for fixing it?
- Standards: What standards are in place for the metadata and its distribution? On the sound recording side, there is emerging consensus on what identifiers should accompany tracks through the digital supply chain. On the publishing side, it's still the Wild West.
- Oversight: What bodies are responsible for ensuring metadata is handled correctly? Who is responsible for certifying that music creators are properly paid for all varieties of use?
- Tracking and matching: Who is responsible for identifying tracks and matching them to consumption (plays or downloads)? Who is required to produce reporting, and in what formats? Which entities calculate and distribute royalties to music creators based on underlying metadata and information on royalty splits?

Minimum Viable Data

Had there been an intelligent plan (or any plan) to transition from a physical media–based music industry to a digital one, we'd surely be better positioned to deal with the massive increase in online music consumption. It's been more than twenty years since Napster, yet even today, record labels, publishers, digital distributors, PROs, and services have different approaches to managing music data, as well as varying comfort levels regarding technology. Inefficiencies in the digital supply chain and a lack of confidence in royalties accounting are the predictable result.

The problem isn't going to fix itself; in fact, absent a comprehensive solution for tracking usage and identifying music rights holders, it's likely to get worse. Allen Bargfrede, head of Berklee College of Music's Rethink Music project, points to a "colossal volume of daily new releases and trillions of streams resulting in increased complexity and a tangled web of royalty structures, rates that differ per territory, and multiple rights owners of songs and assets."⁶ In such an environment, "data has become king."⁷ Complicating matters are changes in copyright ownership as a result of catalog acquisitions and mergers. All of which is why, according to Bargfrede, "owners and users need to be able to synchronize data in multi-party environments that work like streaming at the speed of digital." This requires information that is not only accurate at upload but also remains so across the digital supply chain, even as new data—such as writer splits and copublishing arrangements—is added.

To prevent the garbage in, garbage out problem, it's necessary to establish informational standards for sound recordings and musical works that are distributed digitally. Digital music entrepreneur Benji Rogers calls this "minimum viable data" or MVD, which he describes as "the most essential functions of identifying the original and current owner(s) of a composition or master, and the match of the correct master to the correct composition."⁸ MVD on the sound recording side includes (but is not limited to):

- Track title
- Performing artist(s)
- Album title
- Distributing label
- ISRC code
- UPC code

Pretty straightforward, right? Unfortunately, there are any number of sound recordings floating around without one or another of these identifiers. I've even seen tracks distributed for commercial use that are missing the artist name or have the album field as TBD! Track title, artist, album title, and label shouldn't require any further explanation; in case you're unfamiliar with the last two terms (ISRC and UPC), let me unpack them.

ISRC stands for international standard recording code—a twelve-character string that includes identifiers for country, registrant, year of reference, and a unique designation code for each specific recording. ISRC codes are used widely to track and match usage to sound recordings, but there are still plenty of audio tracks without them. It's easy enough to get an ISRC—if you're on a label or use a digital distributor (or "indie aggregator" like CD Baby, Tunecore, or Distrokid), you most likely won't even have to think about it, as ISRCs are assigned to your tracks before distribution. If you need to obtain ISRC codes yourself, you can do so at the RIAA-managed site https://usisrc.org.

UPC stands for universal product code. No doubt you're familiar with the black-and-white vertical lines and string of numbers emblazoned on everything from bubble gum to boutique vinyl. Unlike ISRC, which represents individual sound recordings, UPC stamps your music as an entire physical or digital product. UPC is what physical and digital retailers use to track sales; most won't handle your release without one. Every product variant requires its own code (single version, album version, remix, remaster, etc.), which is a good thing when it comes to tracking commercial activity for specific recordings or merchandise. In North America, UPC codes are twelve digits (a similar thirteen-digit identifier called EAN13 is used in the United Kingdom). The first six numbers on a UPC code tie back to the manufacturer, the next five relate to the specific item, and the final number is known as the "check digit." Again, if you're on a label or use an established distributor or aggregator, chances are you're all set. If you need or want to obtain your own UPC code, you can do so at https://www.gs1us.org.

To be clear: The MVD described here is by no means the only information that can accompany a sound recording; there are commercial metadata providers and standards bodies such as the Digital Data Exchange (DDEX) that facilitate a range of identifiers useful to sound recording distribution. In the interest of space, I can't get into all of them here, but https://ddex.net has information on metadata configuration well beyond the minimum.

MVD is also crucial for tracking and paying for the use of the underlying compositions embodied in sound recordings, aka publishing. Did I mention that this is a bit of a mess? As previously noted, a big part of the reason why is that musical works can have multiple coauthors and copublishers (I counted ten writers on a recent Ariana Grande hit). Often the biggest music publishers will compel or strongly encourage its writers to collaborate, which can make it easier to identify who controls a musical work (Universal Music Group controls the Ariana Grande track). Still, from a metadata and royalties perspective, the more complex the splits, the more opportunities there are to miss key data. There is a numerical identifier for musical works called the international standard musical work code, though it is less broadly used than its sound recording counterpart, ISRC. The biggest issue with musical works metadata is that songwriter splits aren't always assigned before a sound recording embodying an underlying composition is distributed. The ability to update metadata across the music supply chain with new information is crucial, as is having authoritative databases where this information can be easily obtained and ingested for data matching and royalties processing. There has never been a single comprehensive database for musical works ownership and songwriter splits, though many hope the Mechanical Licensing Collective, established by the 2018 Music Modernization Act will eventually serve this purpose. Let's now review historic attempts to create comprehensive music databases and emerging technologies to tackle the challenge.

The Great Database Race

Well, calling it a race is misleading. More like a series of stumbles toward a goal that some of the biggest corporations in music didn't even acknowledge until fairly recently. A public database (or databases) with information on music ownership would require rights holders to enumerate what they own, as well as agree—along with other stakeholders—to a set of metadata standards. Doing so would maximize efficiency in matching and reporting on usage as well as distributing revenue to every party legally authorized to collect any portion. Specifically, the ingredients for a transparent and equitable digital music ecosystem are

- industry standard metadata that is supported across databases;
- unique, global identifiers for copyrights, sound recordings, and musical works;
- databases with maintained, accurate information regarding these identifiers;
- databases that are interoperable (that is, that "talk to" other databases) to provide a complete ownership picture; and
- databases that are machine readable (that is, that do not require time-intensive human authentication and cross-referencing).

There is considerable work involved in taking inventory of copyrights and preparing music for the digital supply chain. After decades of mergers and acquisitions, the three corporations that control the majority of the planet's recorded music may not have a full comprehension of what they actually own, to say nothing of standardized metadata assigned to these holdings. For their part, smaller labels and publishers may lack the technical aptitude or resources to get their data ducks in a row. Still, there is no doubt that quality music metadata and accessible information on ownership is essential to a functioning twenty-first-century music economy.

I first encountered smart people talking about comprehensive music databases at the turn of the millennium. I recall asking a panel of music technologists at one conference when we might expect such a database to arrive. "In about five years," I was told. I put the same question forward many times over the subsequent decade and always got the same answer. That five years has now become twenty. To be fair, there have been a few attempts by stakeholders to codevelop authoritative, public-facing databases for music data.[9] Unfortunately, none of them have gotten off the ground. Though there are some truly innovative companies doing great work to clean up the digital music industry, the problem with these solutions is that they tend to be proprietary systems with idiosyncratic standards and incomplete information on fractional ownership due to the fact that only one artist or rights holder may be clients of the company.

Enter the Blockchain

There are as many debates about the best type of systems to host music data as there are about data standards. Blockchain is a promising technology that some say holds the key to a more transparent and efficient music industry. Blockchain has taken on near-mythical proportions in the minds of many in the media, technology, and financial industries. Let's look at why.

At its most basic, blockchain is a decentralized, open database that records transactions in an online ledger comprising "blocks" of information. Instead of having a central administrator, a blockchain's "distributed ledger" contains evolving datasets that are synchronized online and visible to those within a network. These networks can have restricted membership, like a corporate intranet, or they can be accessible to anyone, like the public Internet. When a transaction occurs, it is stored in a protected block with other recent events and updated through the entire network. Because information in a blockchain can only be updated but never deleted, it retains a history of changes that may aid in resolving cross-claims or other disputes. Many people associate blockchain with cryptocurrencies like Bitcoin, which similarly utilizes a decentralized ledger. But a music blockchain doesn't have to be married to invisible Internet money with wild value fluctuations and a reputation for illicit transactions. It can piggyback on other kinds of ledgers, or it can be its own system.

With blockchain, a comprehensive music rights system is perhaps easier to envision. MVD assigned to tracks in the blockchain would include a track's title, album, performers, record labels, publishers, writers, PROs, producers, engineers, and mixers. The possibilities go beyond music metadata. Blockchain can provide for licensing options, maintain so-called smart contracts, and contain audio fingerprinting to track fan engagement or link back to information on ownership. Another fundamental aspect of blockchain is that it is nearly impossible to hack. Changes to underlying data relevant to a composition or recording "can only be suggested by trusted parties and approved by owners," according to Verifi Media, a company at the forefront of music blockchain development.

There are currently a lot of smart folks trying to figure out ways that blockchain can resolve the music industry's longstanding issues with transparency and accountability. In 2016, Imogen Heap partnered with developers Ujo and Etherium to release what appears to be the very first song distributed via blockchain. This event was kind of like the moon landing for music tech nerds. And there have been other experiments since, though none have reached anything resembling mass scale. That could change, as there are now dozens of new companies promising to solve the industry's persistent issues with royalties and reporting using some type of blockchain technology. Whether any of these companies succeed depends on more than just the technology itself—real transformation will need to come from the top, with the heads of multinational music corporations choosing to use blockchain as part of their catalog management and distribution strategies. Given these companies' historic resistance to data standardization and searchable ownership repositories, it probably won't happen overnight. There are also potential issues with blockchain that go beyond adoption. We'll consider some of these now.

Music Blockchain Challenges

The first issue is reputational. Blockchain technology is associated with cryptocurrency, which has seen its share of bad actors who have used it to commit fraud, trade in illicit goods and services, or in speculative get-rich-quick schemes. It is important to remember that cryptocurrencies are only one application of blockchain. Still, decision makers may nevertheless be skeptical of the technology based on a misunderstanding of the technology's function and utility. Understanding these distinctions is necessary for music leaders to feel comfortable adopting blockchain. More education is clearly needed.

Music CEOs are also fearful of disruption, having experienced so much of it over the past two decades. Blockchain may be seen as yet another unproven technology that nevertheless threatens the status quo and their place within it. It represents an entirely different way of doing things that at first blush seems ideologically incompatible with the way the music industry has functioned for the better part of a century. Blockchain requires trust in a decentralized system, as opposed to a top-down approach to asset management. Loss of control is still a real worry for music executives whose careers began before the Internet.

And no matter how you slice it (I'm thinking tiny blocks), we're talking about an immature technology. Blockchain has a kind of chicken-and-egg problem: in order for its benefits to be fully realized, it needs to operate at considerable scale. But scalability requires mass participation, which is thus far elusive. Part of the problem is technical: current systems used by the world's largest banks can process transactions at thousands per second. The fastest blockchain, which powers Bitcoin, can process three to seven transactions per second. Etherium, which is already powering some music ledger activity, can handle up to twenty transactions per second. Clearly, there's some catching up to do.

This so-called productivity paradox can't be solved without considerable processing power. And that requires energy. A lot of it. The current energy expenditure for Bitcoin exceeds the energy consumption of some entire nations (looking at you, Liechtenstein). This energy is almost entirely drawn from fossil fuels, which means a fully functional music blockchain could come with an unseemly carbon footprint. This at a time when musicians and music executives alike are embracing green technologies as part of good global citizenship. Mitigation strategies are important to consider before converting millions and millions of global music transactions to blockchain-based systems. Which isn't to say blockchain should be abandoned based on its current energy profile, but rather that it's important to go into this with eyes open to ensure that a blockchain-powered music industry is sustainable.

CONCLUSION

As you are no doubt now aware, solving the music industry's many issues around copyright identification and the distribution of royalties will take a great deal of foresight and no small amount of effort. The former is too often in short supply in this business, and the latter tends to happen only where there is clear financial reward. In some ways, this is why I am hopeful: the biggest music rights holders are seemingly coming around to the idea that they're leaving more money on the table by not having transparent, standardized systems for music data than they manage to extract from black boxes. For its part, the U.S. government must allocate resources to the Library of Congress and Copyright Office to ensure that the official registration body is keeping pace with technological developments and plays a role in establishing and maintaining standards for private market participants. This may seem like a tall order given current realities, but it is essential to an equitable music industry built on the values of creativity, innovation, and economic reward.

8

MUSIC LICENSING

PROs, Publishing Administration, Synchronizations, and More

The whole purpose behind copyright is to give authors of expressive works the ability to profit from their creativity. Music licensing is the granting of permission to use a musical work or sound recording, typically for a fee. As previously discussed, some kinds of music licenses are "compulsory" in that there is federal legislation that compels a certain kind of payment for a certain kind of use, with government oversight in rate setting. Here I'll describe how compulsory/statutory licenses work in more detail and provide information on the Performance Rights Organizations (PROs) that collect and distribute money for these uses. Then I'll outline a few approaches to publishing administration with a focus on the mechanical license. Last, I'll describe so-called synchronization and master use licensing, whereby music copyright owners can earn revenue when their work is used in television shows, motion pictures, advertisements, video games, and other mixed-media projects. Specifically, I'll cover:

- Which PROs are responsible for collecting royalties for performances of musical works, and how to choose and register
- More on SoundExchange, the PRO for noninteractive performances of sound recordings
- Mechanical licenses and publishing administration

- Licensing for television, motion picture, advertising, video games, and other media

It's important to note that music licensing can be complex, competitive, and sometimes counterintuitive. Licensing laws may differ considerably from country to country, and any contract (especially synchronization and master use agreements) should be reviewed by a qualified attorney before you sign. Having dispensed with this caveat, I'll now describe the main areas of music licensing so you can make informed decisions about exploiting your copyrights in a dynamic and evolving marketplace.

PROs AND LICENSING MUSIC FOR PUBLIC PERFORMANCE

We'll start our overview of music licensing with performance licenses. You'll hear these referred to statutory or compulsory licenses, which refer to the same thing: federal legislation that provides a framework for obtaining the rights necessary to publicly perform music. One example is the 1995 Digital Performance Right in Sound Recordings Act (DPRA), which requires digital radio or radio-like services to pay labels and performers for the noninteractive use of sound recordings. The performance right for musical works is enumerated in Section 106 of the Copyright Act, making licensing and payment "compulsory." However, this right does not function under a statutory framework like the one for sound recordings performed on digital radio. Instead, musical works performances are facilitated via blanket licenses issued by performing rights organizations (PROs). Two of those PROs, ASCAP and BMI, are regulated by the federal government, which is why federal courts set rates for PROs and music users when they fail to agree on royalty fees.

As I described in chapters 4 and 5, performance royalties are owed when a copyrighted work is "performed" to the public. For musical works, aka publishing, performances encompass live concerts, prerecorded music played in public venues, or songs broadcast over the airwaves or transmitted in a noninteractive capacity online. For sound recordings, this right is limited to noninteractive digital transmissions like audio webcasting, algorithmic radio, or cable and satellite radio. We'll begin with PROs that license musical works.

In the United States, there are a handful of PROs that collect and distribute royalties for the public performance of musical works: ASCAP, BMI, SESAC, and a newer, smaller PRO known as GMR. These organizations count thousands of songwriters and publishers among their members and offer fee-based "blanket licenses" to public establishments, radio and television broadcasters, cable companies, and digital radio services. Royalties collected for these uses are then distributed by the PROs to their songwriter and publisher members. Some PROs, like ASCAP and BMI, have open enrollment; others, like SESAC and GMR, are invite only and represent smaller, though no less valuable, repertoires. In most other countries, there is only one performing rights society for musical works, and often the same organization offers mechanical licenses. U.S. PROs have reciprocal agreements with foreign rights societies, but the two biggest—ASCAP and BMI—are legally prohibited from touching mechanicals, so they only deal with performance royalties. Let's now look at how the PROs function and who they serve.

ASCAP

Founded in 1914, the American Society of Composers, Authors and Publishers (ASCAP) is a nonprofit organization that collectively licenses musical works for public performance. It's a big job involving big money: ASCAP's total reported revenue in 2019 was over $1.274 billion. ASCAP has been an industry heavyweight for more than a century and at times has used its market power aggressively. In 1941, the U.S. Department of Justice (DOJ) sued ASCAP for violating the Sherman Antitrust Act. Back then, ASCAP was the main vendor of performance licenses, which gave it and its publisher members tremendous leverage. Shortly after the federal government intervened, and ASCAP "consented" to rules meant to curb its anticompetitive behavior.[1] Under its consent decree, ASCAP must offer licenses to services and venues on equivalent terms, although these licenses are nonexclusive and members of the PROs retain the right to individually license their works. With a blanket license from ASCAP, a radio station can play any composition in the PRO's

11.5 million song repertoire without having to seek permission for each individual work.

ASCAP licenses are available to AM/FM radio and television broadcasters, physical venues, and noninteractive digital services. Songwriters and publishers are allowed to negotiate licenses for individual works outside of the blanket license, but most prefer to work within the PRO system. There are a few good reasons for this:

- PRO blanket licenses are more efficient than individually licensing to users
- PROs know the current rate ceiling, whereas songwriters may not
- PROs know what fees correspond to public performance environments from commercial radio to the local café

Let's now take a closer look at the different PROs operating in the United States.

BMI

BMI, or Broadcast Music Inc., is the largest PRO in America, generating $1.311 billion in revenue in 2020, a $28 million increase over the previous year. BMI entered its own DOJ consent decree in 1941 and is likewise only allowed to license its members' compositions for public performance. BMI owes its existence to the oversized influence of ASCAP. At the time of BMI's founding in 1939, radio stations were in a cold war with ASCAP, which they accused of predatory pricing and other abuses of market power. And so a consortium of broadcasters formed BMI as an alternative. Which makes it somewhat ironic that the "new" PRO was slapped with a consent decree a mere two years from its founding. Today, BMI operates as a nonprofit, representing some seventeen million musical works and more than a million songwriters and publishers.

As required by law, BMI offers blanket licenses on similar terms as ASCAP and, like the other regulated PRO, distributes royalties to its members under a 50/50 publisher/songwriter split.

SESAC

Considerably smaller than ASCAP or BMI, the Society of European Stage Authors and Composers (SESAC) is at this time unregulated by the government. The second-oldest American PRO, SESAC was founded in 1930 to promote underserved European authors of dramatic and musical works before evolving to facilitate performance licensing for American songwriters and composers from a range of genres. SESAC counts around thirty thousand songwriter members with one million musical works in its repertoire. A for-profit corporation, SESAC was acquired by the private equity firm The Blackstone Group in 2017.

Due to the fact that it doesn't operate under a consent decree, SESAC has the advantage of being able to offer other licenses beyond public performance (though performance licensing constitutes the bulk of its activity). Becoming a member of SESAC requires an invitation from its creative staff; with superstar songwriters like Bob Dylan and Adele among the SESAC roster, competition is stiff for lesser-known composers. SESAC had previously taken over the mechanical rights licensing body Harry Fox Agency in 2015 and is today one of the main technology vendors for the Mechanical Licensing Collective established by the 2018 Music Modernization Act (MMA).

GMR

Even more exclusive is Global Music Rights (GMR), a boutique PRO founded in 2013 by music attorney and manager Irving Azoff. GMR is the first PRO to come along in seventy-five years, but it is already making waves. Never one to shy away from confrontation, Azoff has taken his formidable negotiation skills directly to services that perform musical works on behalf of a small but celebrated roster of songwriters including Bruce Springsteen, John Lennon, Don Henley of the Eagles, James Hetfield of Metallica, and other heavy hitters.

GMR is invite only, so you'll need hits under your belt to be noticed by Azoff and his well-connected compatriots. With the vast majority of songwriters and composers fenced off from joining, it's unclear whether GMR represents real competition in the PRO marketplace. Still, if

America's youngest PRO can keep enticing high-value songwriters to join, it's poised to make a long-term impact on the licensing market for musical works.

HOW THE PRO SYSTEM WORKS

Musical works PROs are powered by blanket licenses offered to radio and televisions stations, concert venues, and all other establishments that perform music (live or prerecorded). Fees vary depending on the licensee's business; broadcasters typically pay a percentage of gross revenue (around 2.5 percent), but the more revenue a station makes from advertising, the more money PROs can collect. If a station has licenses from ASCAP, BMI, SESAC, and GMR—and most do—it can play pretty much any published song for the period of time covered by the license. It's a pretty efficient system from the licensing side, though not without its conflicts and controversies. PROs negotiate blanket licenses based on what they believe to be the importance of their repertoire to the broadcaster's business. Stations obviously want to pay less, and parties often end up in rate court. (This is also true of digital services that use PRO repertoire.) The MMA changed how royalty fees are determined for the regulated PROs. Previously, the Southern District Court of New York judges had one judge for ASCAP and one for BMI who ruled on rate-setting disputes. The MMA established a "rotating bench" of judges assigned for each new legal embroilment. The regulated PROs welcomed this change as they believe it gives them a better chance at receiving favorable rates in adjudication.

CHOOSING A PRO

Becoming a member of ASCAP and BMI is relatively straightforward. Songwriters in the United States are allowed to be members of only one PRO at a time; they are free to join a different society once their current affiliation term expires. Publishers are allowed to be members of multiple PROs at the same time and usually are. Why? Because it's more efficient for publishers to receive their half of royalties directly from the

PRO that pays the writers' share, especially when a song's cowriters may not belong to the same PRO. Registrations of a work can come from any songwriter, composer, or publisher with a percentage of rights to the work. One registration is sufficient to cover all other claimants, meaning if the publisher submits a registration, the writer doesn't have to. They still can, however. The PROs will record splits based on what the initial filant describes; check the ASCAP and BMI websites for information on how they resolve registration conflicts.

So which PRO should you choose? One can argue the merits of each, but at the end of the day it comes down to which PRO a writer feels will serve her best. If an invite to SESAC or GMR isn't on offer, that leaves BMI and ASCAP to choose from. Both PROs pay 50 percent of royalties owed for the noninteractive plays of repertoire to writers and 50 percent to publishers, but actual payments can vary between PROs based on how they "weight" performances along with other factors, such as bonuses that kick in after a certain number of plays. All PROs deduct anywhere between 11 and 13 percent from royalties owed to cover administrative expenses, which may or may not inform your choice.

There are any number of other reasons a songwriter might pick one PRO over another. In some instances, it's member benefits like educational seminars, mentoring opportunities, discounts on third-party services (think rental cars or subscriptions to industry trade magazines), or other forms of support. Customer service is also important—how responsive is a PRO in responding to inquiries or solving problems? If you're a songwriter, it never hurts to talk to your peers about their experiences. Just know that ASCAP and BMI fulfill the same basic functions, so opinions about how good they are at it are subjective.

For some, earning potential is a crucial factor. Depending on where a song is played and how big a hit it is, PRO payments can differ somewhat. This is in part due to the methodologies used to calculate royalties (all PROs will claim their system is the best). The reality is that the amount of royalties paid will vary based on payment formulas and how each PRO treats certain types of plays. Generally, a song broadcast on a major metropolitan radio station at rush hour is worth more than the Sunday morning graveyard shift. The theme song of a highly rated network television show is worth more than a public access channel performance. Both ASCAP and BMI offer hit song bonuses, so if you have any of those, congratulations and keep up the good work! At the end of the day, revenue from any PRO is informed by the type of music you compose, where that music is performed, and even the stage of your career.

PRO ROYALTY FORMULAS

Each PRO has their own approach to calculating royalties, and they don't always make their methodology easy to understand. For radio, PROs rely on airplay data from any number of playlist tracking services such as MediaBase, Media Monitors, and Broadcast Data Systems, which help PROs know what songs are played on scientifically selected radio stations. When a play is matched to information the PRO has in its computer systems, the writer and publisher receive their share of revenue from the PRO's license fee pool. For example, if a song receives .00123 percent of overall airplay in a royalty period, the PRO will distribute .00123 percent of royalties split between writer(s) and publisher(s). It's important to remember that songs can have multiple cowriters, in which case the song's creators need to determine the splits, and they or their publisher(s) will need to provide that information to their respective PROs.

Television Broadcasts

Television is tracked and calculated differently than radio. The money paid to writers and publishers for TV broadcasts are allocated according to what's known as cue sheets. These contain information on the production, including the name of the program or film, the episode number if it's a show, and all of the music contained therein. The "music cues" in a cue sheet should have detailed information on the writers, publishers, type of use, and duration of use. When the program is broadcast, the PRO matches what's on the cue sheet to their membership roster. To ensure proper tracking and matching, songwriters and publishers should obtain copies of cue sheets containing their music to review for accuracy. Often the publisher will also submit the cue sheet to their PROs, even though it's technically the TV producer's responsibility. Performances of musical works on TV are identified based on airdate schedules and the information contained in the cue sheets using census methodology. For syndicated television, PROs sometimes use sampling methodology, whereby select airings are used as a proxy for overall usage.

Venues and Public Establishments

PROs also collect money from public establishments that use live or prerecorded music. This can include everything from sports arenas, gyms, restaurants, cafés, hotels, and funeral homes to anywhere else where music is played in public. Historically, it has been unfeasible to track individual performances in every venue or establishment, so PROs employ what they call "nonsurveyed" methodology that uses more precisely tracked media like radio and TV to determine what was likely to have been performed in physical spaces. Money from blanket licenses issued to establishments goes into the payable royalty pool, with royalties apportioned using the aforementioned proxies. Unfortunately, this means that smaller songwriters are less likely to receive meaningful income from establishments than, say, Paul McCartney. However, both ASCAP and BMI allow performing songwriters to submit setlists, which theoretically aids the PROs in paying members more accurately for live performances, at least.

Note: While songwriters are encouraged to report what they perform as artists, they are never responsible for paying public performance royalties—it's always the venue's responsibility to obtain a blanket license from the PROs.

You've likely heard business owners complain about the PROs' heavy hand when it comes to pushing blanket licenses. Setting aside the validity of these criticisms, if you operate a public business and believe you don't need to pay for the songs played in your establishment, allow me to disabuse you of that notion. This is one area where some have chosen to fight the law, and the law has conclusively won. Again, I'm not making any claim about the system's inherent fairness but merely letting you know that the legal history strongly favors the PROs. Check the websites of the PROs for more information on fees, which are typically related to the type of use (live performance, karaoke, jukebox, prerecorded CDs or playlists, etc.) and venue occupancy. There are also third-party subscription services such as Pandora Business, Cloud Cover Music, and

Rockbot that offer background music for retail, restaurants, and the like where royalties are prepaid as part of the service.

SIGNING UP WITH A PRO

U.S. PROs all have reciprocal agreements with foreign societies, so it's not necessary for songwriters to sign up with every PRO on the planet. That said, in some instances it may make sense for a foreign writer to sign up directly with a U.S. PRO and vice versa in order to receive direct payments more quickly and without losing additional percentages from administrative fees. If you suspect your songs are being performed in other territories, you can ask your PRO (or prospective PRO) for information on how often royalties are distributed under their reciprocal agreements.

If you are the sole songwriter and also control the publishing, you are eligible to receive 100 percent of royalties minus administrative deductions. ASCAP requires self-published songwriters to sign up separately as the songwriter and the publisher. It's easy enough to do; you can simply make up a publishing name (like Casey's Cool Tunes) as a "doing business as" or d.b.a. Alternatively, you could set up an actual publishing company (LLC is a common designation), which is somewhat more involved. Having done one or the other, ASCAP will deliver both the writer's share and the publisher's share to songwriters for musical works they composed and to which they retain rights. BMI, on the other hand, allows self-published writers to sign up without declaring a publishing company and will send all royalties owed minus administration deductions in one deposit.

With any PRO sign-up, it helps to have pertinent information ready in advance. This includes Social Security number or EIN, bank routing numbers, Tax ID, and information necessary to identify your repertoire (which you already know is called metadata). ASCAP and BMI's online sign-up systems require more or less the same information to set up and facilitate writer and publisher accounts. ASCAP charges a one-time application fee of $50 for writers and publishers (if you're wearing both hats, you'd pay $100). BMI membership is free for songwriters; individual publishers pay $150, while corporate publishers pay $250.

RECENT LEGAL DEVELOPMENTS WITH ASCAP AND BMI

In recent years, some large publishers have attempted to withdraw *only* their digital performance rights from the PROs in order to license directly with services. Their stated reason for doing so is that they believe they can win higher rates in direct negotiation with online music companies. Both the BMI and the ASCAP judges concluded that under the consent decrees, a publisher is either "all in or all out" with regard to their PRO repertoire. Meaning, if they want to pull their digital rights to negotiate directly, they will need to remove their entire catalog from ASCAP or BMI. This is one reason publishers asked the DOJ to modify the consent decrees to explicitly allow partial withdrawal. The DOJ looked at this issue in its Obama-era review of the ASCAP and BMI consent decrees and chose to leave the consent decrees in place and as written.

Another issue that came up in the course of that inquiry was "fractional licensing." Establishments and services have long held the position that if portions of a song belong to both ASCAP and BMI, they only need to obtain a license from one in order to perform the entire work. Publishers (and some songwriters) believed otherwise. Ultimately, the DOJ determined fractional licensing to be impermissible. The Southern District Court of New York disagreed, so for now, broadcasters and venues are obligated to obtain separate blanket licenses from each PRO that controls *any* portion of a song (figure 8.1).

During the Trump administration, the DOJ undertook *another* extensive review of the ASCAP and BMI consent decrees and once again chose to keep things as they are. I don't expect the PROs and publishers to push the Biden DOJ to conduct a third inquiry, but crazier things have happened.

SOUNDEXCHANGE: THE OTHER PRO

Is SoundExchange a PRO? Technically yes, as the nonprofit is tasked by the government with collecting and distributing performance royalties. However, as previously described, SoundExchange is limited to facilitating the statutory license for digital, noninteractive performances of sound recordings only—it is not permitted to license any other uses of sound recordings (such as distributions or synchronizations) and bypasses publishing completely. Another thing SoundExchange doesn't do is collect royalties from AM/FM radio. Remember, a loophole in federal law allows terrestrial broadcasters to not pay a dime to artists and labels for over-the-air plays of their audio tracks.

In chapter 5, I described how the 1995 Digital Performance Right in Sound Recordings Act (DPRA) established a limited performance right for sound recordings and led to the creation of SoundExchange. Under the DPRA, a trio of federal judges called the Copyright Royalty Board (CRB) sets rates for various categories of service (webcasting, cable and satellite radio), considering evidence and determining royalties for various categories of noninteractive service for a five-year period. (The CRB also sets rates for mechanical royalties, as described in chapter 4.) Recall that royalties are paid by SoundExchange to performers and labels under 50/45/5 percent splits, whereby the sound recording owner (typically the label, but sometimes the artist) gets 50 percent, the featured performer gets 45 percent, and 5 percent goes to background singers and musicians. SoundExchange takes an additional administrative fee of around 5 percent, which is considerably lower than musical works PROs. Like those entities, SoundExchange has reciprocal agreements

Figure 8.1. U.S. Performing Rights Organizations (PROs).

with royalties societies outside the United States, where the digital performance right is typically referred to as "neighboring rights." So if you're feeling worldly, you can think of SoundExchange as America's neighboring rights society.

How SoundExchange Works

Royalties are paid to artists and labels separately; labels don't touch the performers' portion unless the label has a direct deal with a service, in which case they are responsible for paying performers' shares to their artists. As noted, SoundExchange *only* collects royalties for public performances of sound recordings on noninteractive digital services. That's not iTunes, and that's not Spotify. Services that *do* perform music in a noninteractive capacity are music webcasters, algorithmic "radio" apps, cable radio (those nonvideo music channels at the high end of your cable dial), and satellite radio (SiriusXM). Many interactive services operate digital radio "bolt-ons" but acquire the majority of the necessary performance rights directly as part of their distribution deals with the labels; the remainder is paid to SoundExchange via statutory license. (Refer to chapter 5 for more information on copyright and sound recording distributions.)

Signing Up with SoundExchange

Unless you have a direct deal with the aforementioned noninteractive services, the only way to get paid for digital performances of sound recordings is through SoundExchange. Therefore it is crucial to register if your tracks are being performed on digital radio. These days, more and more artists retain ownership of their masters, which means they are eligible to collect 95 percent of royalties owed (minus the union deduction). For much of SoundExchange's history, artists had to sign up as performer and "label" if they owned their masters. This was a separate process, and I can't tell you how many artist rights holders I've talked to who didn't even know it was an option. Which means 50 percent of their royalties probably went into a black box. Recently, SoundExchange created an option in its online registration process for artists to choose both performer and sound copyright owner with a single click.

Keep in mind that this option only applies to tracks for which the artist is the performer *and* owns the sound recording. Any tracks on which a featured artist performs that are owned by other entities will result in 45 percent going to the performer and 50 percent of royalties to the respective label owner(s).

To sign up, go to SoundExchange.com; registration is free and relatively painless. You'll want to have your ID handy, though, as SoundExchange requires valid identification to successfully process an application. The online form has a helpful feature that takes a photo of your government-issued ID. If you're a member of a musical group or groups, you can list them, along with the percentage of royalties you claim for sound recording performances. (It's smart for bands to have these discussions ahead of time.) The process is similar for rights owners only, whether individuals or corporations. Once the basic information is registered, it's time to list your sound recording catalog. Entering proper metadata is essential to getting paid, so be sure to double and triple check your work (check chapter 7 for more detail on sound recording metadata).

MECHANICAL ROYALTIES, THE MUSIC LICENSING COLLECTIVE, AND PUBLISHING ADMINISTRATION

Having gone into considerable detail about mechanical royalties in chapter 4, I'll focus now on the "how" of managing this right, with an emphasis on solutions for self-published songwriters. Going forward, the expectation is that some number of independent and unaffiliated songwriters will sign up with the Mechanical Licensing Collective (MLC) established by the 2018 MMA. The MLC officially launched just as this book was going to press; it remains to be seen whether it can deliver on its promise to simplify mechanical licensing and get more writers paid. I personally hope so, but it's also worthwhile to examine other options for mechanical license issuance and administration.

HARRY FOX AGENCY

The Harry Fox Agency (HFA) was founded way back in 1927 by the National Music Publishers Association, who ran the organization for decades. The publishers sold HFA to SESAC in 2015, right around the time reports were surfacing about HFA's mechanical licenses with Spotify not covering a bunch of repertoire Spotify believed it did. (SESAC itself was acquired by private equity firm Blackstone in 2017.) To this day, HFA offers mechanical licenses to services like Spotify, paying royalties to its publisher members based on reported usage.

HFA will only accept publishers whose musical works have been embodied in sound recordings officially released by labels, so it's never been a great solution for performing songwriters who self-release their sound recordings. Nevertheless, in 2019 HFA was brought on to help run the MLC. This is a curious arrangement, considering a big reason the MLC came to be in the first place was because HFA could not provide Spotify and other interactive services with end-to-end mechanical rights coverage. In fact, it was mostly independent songwriters and publishers that fell through the cracks—the folks least likely to be included in HFA's database. Still, it behooves self-published songwriters who don't already have publishing administration to sign up with the MLC. Otherwise, their money goes into yet another black box. Songwriters signed with major publishers may not see much benefit from the new collective as the Big Three are likely to continue licensing directly with the services.

SIGNING UP FOR THE MECHANICAL LICENSING COLLECTIVE

Before signing up with the MLC it's important to note that the collective only pays self-published songwriters directly; songwriters who have signed their musical works copyrights to a publisher will continue to be paid by their publisher according to their two-party contract. (As described in chapter 4, that's typically a 50/50 split postrecoupment of writer advances.)

The last time I looked at the MLC website (themlc.com), I encountered an array of hard-to-parse infographics and too-cute-by-half music buzzwords. The goal, as I understand it, is to get songwriters, who may not fully understand what mechanical royalties are, to sign up for the new system. This may prove challenging. I say this as someone who spent quite a few years advising recording artists to sign up for SoundExchange. Do I sound cynical? Probably. But if you're a self-releasing recording artist who writes their own songs and doesn't have publishing administration, it's still a good idea to register.

The MLC registration "portal," Connect to Collect, is described as the "first step" to receiving mechanical royalties sometime down the road. The process involves the creation of a member profile that the MLC says will allow songwriters to

- review detailed information regarding existing works registrations;
- edit those existing works registrations to make sure your data is as accurate as possible;
- create and submit new registrations for musical works not yet registered with the MLC;
- manage and update your contact information, banking instructions, and tax forms; and
- invite other users from your organizations to set up their own user accounts under your MLC member profile.

To do any of this, you'll need to enter some basic contact information (name, address, email, phone, etc.) and wait for an email link that takes you to another page to create a password. A couple of text-based authentications later and you've got your hands on the nuclear codes, I mean, an opportunity to enter *more* information for a member account. After that, you wait one to three days for a follow-up link that will allow you to do the stuff in the previous bullet points. Godspeed, and may your musical works be properly matched to digital service usage reports!

PUBLISHING ADMINISTRATION

Technically, any process where royalties are collected for the use of musical works is "publishing administration." Here I'll focus mainly on reproductions and distributions, which we know as mechanical royalties. Specifically, I am using the term "publishing administration" to describe third-party services that songwriters use to manage their mechanical royalties (and occasionally other rights). Some publishing administration companies offer a suite of services that also include PRO registration and repertoire management as well as synchronizations. Let's look more closely at how this all works.

Indie Aggregators and Standalone Publishing Administration

Many recording artists who self-release their work use "indie aggregators" such as Tunecore or CD Baby to distribute their sound recordings to download stores and interactive streaming services. Both of those companies also offer publishing administration, and a third, Distrokid, plans to launch its own musical works–focused service. There are also standalone publishing administration services like Songtrust (which powers CD Baby's publishing administration, CD Baby Pro Publishing), Sentric, and Audiam. For more established writers, there's Kobalt. One of the biggest advantages of publishing administration companies is that you retain ownership of your copyrights. It also eliminates the need for self-published songwriters to track down their mechanical royalties from services and societies around the world. CD Baby Pro Publishing, Tunecore Publishing, Songtrust, and Centric each claim to collect royalties from more than 215 territories, so coverage is quite comprehensive.

Publishing administration companies are paid in a few different ways. Services can come bundled with sound recording distribution, where an artist pays extra to have royalties collected for the underlying compositions embodied in their sound recordings. Other companies offer publishing administration independent of sound recording distribution. Some services do not charge anything at sign-up, taking a percentage of royalties (anywhere from 15 to 20 percent); others take an up-front fee plus commission.

Some publishing administration services also offer to manage performance royalties and synchronizations. It's important to review the terms closely to make sure this is opt in. My feeling is that it isn't strictly necessary to have them touch your performance royalties because you can sign up with a PRO yourself and they already take a deduction.

Likewise, you may want to retain your synchronization rights. At the least you should make sure an administration company's offer to handle syncs is nonexclusive. One reason is that there is no compulsory license for syncs and direct negotiation may fetch higher fees for certain uses. Publishing administration services will also take anywhere from 40 to 50 percent of the money from song placement. Last, it's not always clear how actively repertoire is promoted, so opportunities may be missed. A browsable library isn't the same as a targeted pitch. All of this might be fine for certain types of music, especially if the sync agreement is nonexclusive. Nevertheless, be sure to check the fine print.

Signing with a Music Publisher

With all of the options available to today's songwriters, why sign with a publisher? There are a few reasons actually:

- Not all songwriters are performing artists.
- Publishers also offer advances.
- Publishers have experience exploiting musical works and negotiating fees for their use.

If your talent is on the composition side, backing from an experienced publisher might make sense. Keep in mind that the world of professional songwriting is highly competitive and major publishers are particularly hit focused. If that's the market you're hoping to compete in, there are advantages to being with a company that can match your songs to recording artists who will make them huge. Let's face it, it's easier to get a song in front of Ariana Grande if you're with the major music company she happens to be signed to (that would be Universal Music Group).

Publishers also offer advances, which are no doubt smaller than in previous decades but can still be meaningful depending on a songwriter's repertoire and ability to crank out future hits. But remember, once you sign the contract, the publisher will own your songs, meaning you'll have less control over how and where they're used. Major publishers may also attempt to limit your collaborations to only songwriters on their roster or set you up with writers with whom you have no established creative affinity. That's just the way the game works at this level. If you're interested in playing it, you'll need your demos to be competitive with what's on commercial radio. It also helps to live in a city where the major publishers have a presence. Historically, that's places like Nashville, New York City, and Los Angeles, but publishers obviously sign writers from all over the world. To be sure, the Internet makes it much easier to send demos to music companies. Yet you're unlikely to get a response unless a connected music attorney or another writer on the roster makes an introduction. This part of the business is still a hustle.

Perhaps the biggest reason to sign with a publisher is that publishers have experience exploiting musical works and negotiating fees for their use. This expertise can't be overlooked, especially because songwriters may not know a song's potential value in various licensing scenarios. A good lawyer or music business manager can also be useful in this regard, but big publishers have entire departments devoted to clearances and placements. That said, independent songwriters (and unsigned recording artists) are often able to clear synchronizations more quickly, which benefits music supervisors working on tight deadlines. And on that note, let's look at the thrilling world of licensing music for other forms of media.

LICENSING FOR FILM, TELEVISION, ADVERTISING, VIDEO GAMES, ETC.

Diminishing returns from the sales of physical media means that artists, songwriters, and music rights holders are seeking out new revenue streams for their recordings and compositions. This includes licensing music for film, television, video games, and advertisements. When I was in bands in the 1990s, the idea of having your music in a commercial was considered by most of my peers as "selling out." I remember what a big deal it was when "1234" by indie singer-songwriter Feist appeared in a 2007 ad for the iPad Nano. That placement was significant in part because Feist had been relatively unknown before the spot scored her a new—and global—audience. It helped that the use was undeniably cool—the opposite of the cringey placements I grew up seeing on network television. Yup, the Feist placement was a big deal. And surely a big paycheck.

Obviously, not all ad placements are as lucrative as an Apple commercial. My point is, there's no longer a stigma when an up-and-coming act licenses their music in this way. These days, getting a song placed is almost a rite of passage. It's definitely a buyer's market, though, and getting more competitive every day. Still, independent artists can and do make real money from music copyright clearance. Maybe your song won't end up in the next Avengers movie (c'mon, there'll be another one), but it might be perfect for a thought-provoking documentary on why superhero movies suck. Consider how many streaming video platforms and apps there are, most with original shows and movies that use music. This pipeline needs content, content, content. Then there's the emerging world of virtual reality, a yet to be saturated market for music licensing.

I should mention that licensing a preexisting composition or recording for use in other media is somewhat different from writing and recording music specifically for a project. The former can be thought of as a "soundtrack" and the latter a "score." Both usually have an associated fee or royalty, but the way music is created and licensed can vary based on the needs of a project. For the most part, I will focus on the licensing of prerecorded music for use in other media. Scores are often works made for hire with music created by in-house or contracted composers, so it falls somewhat outside our area of focus.

And because this is a book about music copyright, I also won't be getting into the psychology of clearances, which is more about trends and customs in this part of the industry. There are plenty of guides out there from folks on both the licensor (rights holder) and licensee (user of the music) side of this business that offer more detail on how media producers select songs and how to build relationships and prepare music for placement. There are also at least a few conferences devoted to the topic. What we need to first understand are what rights are being licensed and how revenue flows from common syncs and master uses. And that's what I've got cued up.

SYNCHRONIZATIONS AND MASTER USE LICENSES

As you should now be well aware, the two copyrights in music have different licensing frameworks. When it comes to music used in other media, the process for both copyrights is similar. This is because using music in this way always requires permission from the rights holders. Unless the same party fully controls the rights to both the sound recording and underlying composition, the licensee must obtain clearances from all parties with a claim to any portion of the work. On the publishing side, mixed media uses are called synchronizations, or syncs. On the sound recording side, they're called master uses (and sometimes, colloquially, syncs).

The "licensor" is the party or parties who own whatever portion of a music copyright—this can be artists, labels, songwriters, or publishers. The "licensee" is the party seeking to use music in another form of media. The individual who tries to make it happen on behalf of directors or producers is known as a music supervisor. The music supervisor may or may not choose the music, but they will always seek the most expeditious and least expensive route to "locking in" a placement. That music supervisors tend to move at the speed of light gives a leg up to rights holders who can quickly clear both "sides." Artists who write their own songs and retain rights for their compositions and recordings are in a position to clear everything in one swoop. This is known as "one-stop" licensing. And if a track is right for a project, music supervisors always prefer it.

It's also not unheard of for a music supervisor to license a new recording of a song originally popularized by another artist in order to save money. An example would be the Beatles, whose recordings are among the most well known and the most expensive to license. While the publishing fees for Beatles's songs are also spendy, licensing a new recording is cheaper than securing rights to both the composition and the original cut. This is why you're more likely to hear a Beatles cover in a movie than the original track. At the end of the day, however, it comes down to how badly a producer or director wants a specific performance of a specific song. For one episode of "Mad Men," show creator Matthew Weiner got AMC to pay a reported $250,000 to license the Beatles's "Tomorrow Never Knows" because he felt the song was essential to a scene. This is true for pretty much all syncs: what matters most is whether a track works. Next is how much it costs, and how quickly it can be locked in.

TYPES OF PLACEMENTS AND FEE RANGES

Commercials

Advertisers can pay anywhere from a thousand to half a million bucks for the use of sound recordings and compositions in their campaigns. Here it's often less important that an artist is well known than the song having the right feel and message. Typically, music in advertisements is upbeat, friendly, and optimistic—whatever inspires a viewer to feel positively about a product or service. Sometimes the vibe is edgy, flirty, or adventurous. It's easy enough to follow trends in national ad campaigns; one year everything will sound like Arcade Fire, the next, it'll be the Lumineers or the Black Keys. If you are willing and able to record music that corresponds to commercial trends, you've got a better shot of placement. There's no point trying to place a death metal track where a firm wants ukuleles.

Movie Trailers

It's common for a song to be used in a movie trailer but not in the actual movie. This is because trailers are advertisements for the movie and not the film itself. Trailers evoke the emotional or narrative qualities of the movie they're promoting in a compressed amount of time. Epic-sounding tracks or tunes that tug on the heartstrings are de rigueur. Paydays can be considerable, especially for films the studios hope will do big box office numbers. A single placement can be in the six figures, though smaller, independent projects will offer a good deal less. Trailer music tends to trade on audience familiarity, so unknown songs by unknown acts may not make the cut. However, it's not unheard of for a trailer to feature an up-and-coming performer doing a new take on a well-known song. In fact, there's a whole subtrend of upbeat numbers getting somber makeovers in movie trailers.[2] Maybe there's a home for your cold wave cover of "Dancing Queen" after all.

Motion Pictures

I said I wouldn't get into the psychology of placements, but movies are one place where a song needs to "work" above all else. This can come down to a specific scene and how the music is used in that scene, or it can be an overall aesthetic or "feel" a director is attempting to conjure. David Lynch or Quentin Tarantino, for example, are known to use music by just about any artist in any genre provided it enhances the mood of a scene. "Replaceability" is a factor in movie syncs. If one track works perfectly and nothing else will do, it can result in higher fees. As you'd expect, the bigger the picture, the bigger the payday. Six figures is not uncommon for a key placement in a flick destined for the cineplex. Again, indie films and most documentaries will pay less. If you're lucky, a placement will keep on earning: if the movie ends up being broadcast on television, it will generate performance royalties on the publishing side (see this very chapter for information on how).

Television Shows

You no doubt have noticed the explosion of original content currently being produced for television, delivered as a linear broadcast or on-demand. For music, this spells opportunity. It also means that TV syncs don't pay as well as major motion pictures due to the need to feed the beast. For independent artists, fees can range from gratis (free uses for "exposure") to around $15,000 for a track featured in a prime-time network show. Music supervisors who work in television often pride themselves on breaking new acts, which is sweet for developing artists. Another asset for indies is that music owned by major labels and publishers is usually more expensive to license and clearances can take longer.

Video Games

There seems to be no ceiling for the video game market. As is the case with motion pictures, major game studios put millions of dollars behind their tentpole releases, most of which have a musical score or use prerecorded songs, such as the "radio stations" in Rockstar Games's popular Grand Theft Auto series. Like movies, game release announcements come with trailers that also feature music. There are scores of independent game producers who are always looking for tracks to license. Fees can range from $2,000 to $30,000, depending on the music and the game. Licenses for video games are typically "buyouts," meaning the licensee is able to freely reproduce and distribute a game without having to pay additional royalties. Occasionally, deals will offer a percentage of sales (typically around 10 cents per unit) to music rights holders.

A Note about Podcasts

Speaking of gold rushes, the market for podcasts is on fire, with large companies like Spotify, SiriusXM/Pandora, and others trying to catch up with Apple's established lead in podcast aggregation. There is no compulsory or statutory license for music used in podcasts, which means producers must obtain permission from the owners of the sound recordings and musical works. Again, fees can range from zero dollars into the thousands, depending on audience size and track value. Some podcasts attempt to fly under the radar with music licensing, others—including music-focused podcasts—don't use music at all, use library music, use music produced in-house, or only use snippets of published songs. It's possible that some uses of music in podcasts could be determined "fair" if they were to be litigated. I don't know of any existing case law, however. This means to avoid liability any music used must be licensed.

Sync Agents and Music Libraries

I already mentioned that music supervisors like it when licensing is easy and efficient. Sync agents aim to make that dream a reality. This is an area where self-contained composers have an advantage. Because the idea is efficiency, this is not the business to be in if you have cocomposers. Sync agents do take commissions, typically between 25 and 50 percent of the placement fee. (I'd personally avoid working with companies that take a percentage of your PRO fees.) Music supervisors looking to quickly license musical "beds," "bumpers," or "stingers" (audio events that evoke a mood or establish tension) might turn to sync agents for various kinds of productions. There are also what's known as "music libraries" that offer royalty-free music for anyone to use for a fee or subscription. Music libraries are all about volume (and I don't mean audio levels)—they tend to offer cheap to license music for smaller projects (think wedding videos or corporate training spots).

Exclusive versus Nonexclusive

Most sync and master use licenses these days are nonexclusive. That means you can license the same song to another user without restrictions. Because you're not transferring ownership of the song or recording to the licensee, they are only able to use it in the specific context for which you have negotiated permission and fees. This is why you might hear a popular song in several TV shows or movies within a relatively short period of time. Exclusive licensing agreements are most often found in the world of advertising, where corporate brands often prohibit the use of a track in campaigns for a similar product or forbid licensing to a business competitor. Exclusivity usually means higher fees, which is something to keep in mind when negotiating.

A Note on Copyright Reversion

Much of the previous information presumes that copyright ownership resides with the author of the work(s). If you're signed to a label or a publisher, they will be the ones who make decisions about where your music is exploited. Copyright law does, however, give authors of expressive works the opportunity to recapture their copyrights after thirty-five years. This right, which is known as "termination of transfer" or "copyright termination," was established by Congress in Section 203 of the 1976 Copyright Act. Lawmakers thought it prudent to give creators "another bite of the apple" during the life of copyright (which in the 1976 act was extended from a maximum of fifty-six years to seventy-five years and subsequently extended to the author's life plus seventy years). Sometimes an author will choose to renegotiate rather than retake ownership, which is part of the reason why Congress established the right in the first place. Creators often have less leverage at the beginning of their careers than they do later on, which is something I brought up when testifying before Congress on this issue in 2014.

Reversion is not automatic; authors have a window of time approaching the date of the original transfer during which they must send notice of their intent to terminate to the Copyright Office and the current owner of the work.[3] This can be a complicated maneuver that sometimes results in litigation. Record labels like to pretend that this right doesn't exist, and there is a lack of court precedent around sound recording terminations. (There have been a few important songwriter victories on the publishing side.) All of which to say, it's definitely best to consult with a qualified attorney before attempting to reclaim your previously transferred copyrights.

CONCLUSION

Licensing is where the rubber hits the road with music copyrights. As I have described, some forms of licensing, such as performances of musical works and digital performances of sound recordings, are "set it and forget it"—you pick a PRO, sign-up, and wait for the check to arrive (old timers call it "mailbox money," although these days it's mostly direct deposit). Other kinds of licenses, such as synchronizations and master uses, are more hands-on. Here your ability to derive revenue depends on a host of factors, including the type of music, the market for that type of music, the type of use, and whether that use is exclusive or nonexclusive. It may not make sense to go it alone with these kinds of licenses. If you have questions about deal terms or aren't sure what fees to ask for, you'll want to consult an attorney with negotiating experience. Plenty of folks in the music industry have learned things the hard way, but it's usually nicer if you don't have to.

9

FINAL THOUGHTS

Music Copyright and the Big Picture

By now, you should have a better sense of how music copyright came to be, including its fitful evolution alongside technological innovation. You also understand something of how music copyright functions in practice, which empowers you to more confidently set and achieve goals and protect your interests. Now, I'll zoom out for a bigger picture view of where the industry stands today and where it might be heading. As I do, I'll touch on the core concepts established in prior chapters, but this is really about what kind of future for music copyright we want, expect, or even deserve.

There are many more ways to access music today than at any other time in history. Still, a major challenge for today's music is making enough money to stay in the game even as recording and distribution become more efficient and inexpensive. While a plethora of digital services exist to provide access to unfathomable amounts of music, a relatively small percentage of content generates an overwhelming amount of activity. In the wake of a global pandemic, the recorded music industry is making money hand over fist, with the RIAA reporting more than $10 billion in revenue in 2020.[1] (It's important to acknowledge the massive contraction in the live music sector, but I'm talking about revenue from the exploitation of music copyrights.) As was the case pre-COVID, these earnings are disproportionately driven by back catalog rather than new release music.[2] This gives the biggest music companies a huge advantage in the modern marketplace.

With just three corporations controlling the vast majority of recorded music copyrights, it is easy to see how private market deals can further favor the majors. And I count four mainstream tech companies with an outsized role in distribution and access: Spotify, Apple, Amazon, and Google. As the big labels are increasingly partnered with services in the form of equity ownership, they have access to an incredible amount of data to guide their decisions around investment and positioning and the deal structures to foreclose competition. In some ways, this has always been the business model: leveraging copyrights to maximize value from whatever the distribution pipe happens to be. The question is, who does this serve?

Historically, record labels were risk aggregators, meaning they spread the expenses of producing, distributing, and marketing music across a great many releases and made their money back (and then some) from the few that did very well. They also functioned as a bank for the musicians (with worse terms than most financial institutions), offering advances and tour support with contractual ninjutsu to ensure nonrecoupment. Historic label deals were often onerous, but when things worked, artists had able partners in generating value. Of course, *generating* value is not the same thing as *capturing* value. In the old system, major labels captured most of the value. Depending on an artist's stature, their leverage, and the terms of their contract, today may not be all that much different.

Retaining ownership of your copyrights can be useful in terms of flexibility and responsiveness to an evolving marketplace driven by technology. Still, the core challenge faced by any artist these days is being heard in an incredibly noisy marketplace. Marshaling attention costs gobs and gobs of money. And who has this kind of cash to throw around? Major labels. And what does a risk-averse, twenty-first century imprint look for? Globally bankable superstars. Of course, consolidated multinational music conglomerates aren't the only ones with deep pockets and a will to dominate. Technology companies that have already achieved scale are in a position to determine the contours of distribution in a globally networked market for music. Meanwhile, consumers are conditioned to expect access to everything at any time, as they sail endless seas of apps, ads, and uploads.

I bring this up not as a prognosticator of doom and gloom but rather to contemplate whether the current power dynamics in the music industry honor the spirit of Article 1, Section 8, Clause 8 of the U.S. Constitution, which establishes the essential compact for copyright in America. Recall the explicit and implicit balance struck by this compact: "To promote the progress of science and useful arts, by securing for limited times to authors and inventors the exclusive right to their respective writings and discoveries."

Like the Force in *Star Wars*, copyright is about balance. It's therefore important to look to the inherent tensions in copyright to see if they advance or frustrate "progress" as constitutionally construed. On one hand, it's no longer strictly necessary for authors to enjoy economic reward for creation, if it ever was. Technology gives anyone the ability to fix their expression in a tangible form and disseminate it broadly. But even where money isn't the motivator, copyright gives us a framework with which to respect the intellectual and creative product of others. This tends to get lost in the pitched battles between technology and content. Too often copyright is used as an excuse for no-holds-barred, zero-sum industrial warfare, with governments serving as reluctant and ill-equipped mediators. It doesn't have to be this way. Ultimately, copyright is about authors. It is about the public. It is about the enrichment of our society and the incentive to create. Encouraging respect for these values was a big reason for my writing this book.

Conversations around copyright are becoming increasingly polarized and stakeholders radicalized. In this way, things look a lot like the overall economic and political situation we find ourselves in. Long term, this situation benefits no one—not the public, not the technology platforms, and certainly not the artists, whose livelihoods are ultimately dependent on their ability to access and cultivate audiences and patrons. The promise of copyright is that creators can participate in the marketplace of ideas and enjoy remuneration for works the public deems of value. The promise of the Internet was that creators who previously had few on ramps to reach audiences and fans who had scarcer ways to access music could more efficiently find one another. Both of these promises have in some ways been fulfilled during the haphazard transition to a largely digital economy for music. But the distribution of reward has been anything but equitable.

Some self-styled artist champions often evince apologist attitudes about how it was better back when corporate rights holders ran the roost. You know, the good old days, when artists were forced to play a lottery in order for the chance to have their creations enter the marketplace. A world defined by bottlenecks and gatekeepers in which the mere promise of reaching audiences necessitated a transfer of rights to an outside entity for no less than a statutory term of thirty-five years (and then only under highly specific requirements beyond the administrative ken of most authors and heirs).

A righteous pro-artist agenda would look to the Constitution for guidance on how to structure our creative economies. There is nothing in Article I, Section 8 of the U.S. Constitution that references intermediaries, whether they're multinational content conglomerates or giant technology concerns. Let's put to rest the lie that either side always has creators' interests at heart. Major music companies have historically been less than transparent with their copyright holdings and accounting to music creators. Technology companies also have an unsavory history of exploiting musicians and songwriters without recompense. Tech CEOs and investors have often posed as beneficent purveyors of access while engaging in widespread data harvesting for the purpose of monetizing our every click, swipe, and keystroke.

Even before our lives became mediated by mass-scale social platforms with their endless opportunities for doom scrolling and anonymized invective, there was the issue of unauthorized distribution of copyrighted works, including and especially music. Piracy was and is a scourge, but it is not the whole story. Even if it were eradicated tomorrow, it probably wouldn't change the winner-takes-all dynamics of today's music marketplace. The attention economy demands just that, and those in a position to wield it tend to be large corporations who operate must-participate platforms (social media, streaming, etc.) or those with superstar rosters and massive back catalogs.

Personally, I believe that the content versus tech dichotomy is an illusion, especially in an era of rampant corporate consolidation. People don't go online to experience an efficient digital packet-switching protocol. It's the content (aka copyrights). Copyright conglomerates have more or less successfully transitioned to new business models, often enjoying tremendous influence within existing licensing structures. Music is now a data and service industry, and both "sides" seek the same thing: control over distribution and pricing. When you hear terms like "full-stack integration," it's code for attempts to maximize leverage from ownership to distribution to application to interface to consumer data. This isn't a music versus tech thing. It's a twenty-first-century marketplace thing.

One barrier to reform is that many in music and tech are highly invested in the current system, even as they complain about it. Today, many Internet companies that once championed a streamlined copyright regime have abandoned any grand vision of reform. Why? Because they have achieved scale and are already making gobs of money from data mining, advertising, or other means. Music licensing is mostly a nuisance for the biggest tech concerns, but it helps attract users to their services. These companies seek to maintain an advantage by keeping content acquisition costs down or by advocating for streamlined licensing (and in the case of the Music Modernization Act, occasionally achieving it).

Meanwhile, the content companies, despite their outrage, are making a lot of money through deals with the digital service providers. For too long they have lacked incentive to clean their own house to better serve creators, nor can they reimagine rights and exceptions for fear of giving Internet companies additional leverage. As previously described, there's a dataflow problem in music that impacts how copyrights are exploited and whether creators are paid efficiently or at all. This situation is slowly improving as the realization dawns that enumerating their ownership interests is crucial to not leaving money on the table in a globally networked marketplace. But make no mistake about it: the consolidated music companies and the global digital service providers are in business with one another. And everyone else goes along for the ride according to economic terms set by the biggest interests in music and tech (or the federal government).

Serving the interests of copyright creators at the ground floor means establishing structures and business models to accommodate enterprise at a more modest scale than total global domination. Such efforts would benefit from renewed investment in localism and regionalism, with music education—including copyright—as part of the picture. Business at this level doesn't have to be one size fits all. It can be diverse and tailored to the needs of practitioners, entrepreneurs, and developers. It can make use of technology to produce custom innovations that make sense at a more modest scale. It can harness data to establish working models to export to other communities, where business and civic leaders can truly partner with culture producers to make decisions about implementation in their own burgs and burbs. And the best thing is, this can happen now, with or without major copyright reform.

My advice is to partner with other creative people at whatever level you're at who share your views about sustainability and fairness. This can be developers, artists in other disciplines, local businesses, municipal and state agencies, nonprofits, community media hubs, and educators. Seed your values and tend to their flowering in your own patch, however small. If everyone takes this approach, we have a much better shot at ensuring that copyright serves the interests of authors and the public and not just multinational technology and media companies. After all, the future of music is in all of our hands.

APPENDIX

INDUSTRY AND MUSIC CREATOR ORGANIZATIONS

Americana Music Association (AMA): Trade organization representing the American roots music community, https://americanamusic.org/.
American Association of Independent Music (A2IM): Represents the interests of independent labels, https://a2im.org/.
American Federation of Musicians (AFM): Union representing musicians, https://www.afm.org/.
Artist Rights Alliance (ARA): Music creator advocacy group, https://artistrightsalliance.org/.
Association of Independent Music Publishers (AIMP): Represents the interests of independent music publishers, https://www.aimp.org/.
Christian Music Trade Association (CMTA): Trade organization representing the Christian music community, http://www.cmta.biz/.
Church Music Publishers Association (CMPA): Represents the interests of Christian music publishers, https://cmpamusic.org/.
Country Music Association (CMA): Trade organization representing country music, https://www.cmaworld.com/.
Future of Music Coalition (FMC): Music creator advocacy group, http://futureofmusic.org/.

Gospel Music Association (GMA): Represents the interests of the gospel music community, https://gospelmusic.org/.

International Bluegrass Music Association (IBMA): Represents the interests of the bluegrass music community worldwide, https://ibma.org/.

Music Artists Coalition (MAC): Music creator advocacy group, https://www.musicartistscoalition.com/.

Music Business Association (Music Biz): Music commerce membership body, https://musicbiz.org/.

Music Managers Forum USA (MMF): Represents the interests of U.S. music managers, https://www.mmfus.com/.

Nashville Songwriters Association International (NSAI): Songwriter advocacy group, https://www.nashvillesongwriters.com/.

National Academy of Recording Arts and Sciences (NARAS): Music industry trade association that hosts the Grammys, https://www.grammy.com/recording-academy.

National Music Publishers' Association (NMPA): Represents the interests of major music publishers, https://www.nmpa.org/.

Recording Industry Association of America (RIAA): Represents the interests of major labels, https://www.riaa.com/.

Rhythm and Blues Foundation: Represents the interests of the soul and R&B music community, https://www.rhythmandbluesfoundation.org/.

Screen Actors Guild and AFTRA (SAG-AFTRA): Union representing film and television performers and background singers, https://www.sagaftra.org/.

Songwriters Guild of America (SGA): Songwriter advocacy group, https://www.songwritersguild.com/.

Songwriters of North America (SONA): Songwriter advocacy group, https://www.wearesona.com/.

PERFORMING RIGHTS AND MECHANICAL ROYALTY COLLECTIVES

American Society of Composers, Authors and Publishers (ASCAP): Government-regulated music publishing performance rights society, https://www.ascap.com/.

APPENDIX

Broadcast Music, Inc. (BMI): Government-regulated music publishing performance rights society, https://www.bmi.com/.
Global Music Rights (GMR): Private music publishing performance rights society, https://globalmusicrights.com/.
Harry Fox Agency: Private mechanical licensing society owned by SESAC, https://www.harryfox.com/.
Mechanical Licensing Collective (MLC): Government-regulated mechanical royalties society, https://www.themlc.com/.
SESAC: Private music publishing performance rights society, https://www.sesac.com/.
SoundExchange: Collection society for the digital public performance right in sound recordings, https://www.soundexchange.com/.

LEGISLATIVE, REGULATORY, AND RATE-SETTING BODIES

Copyright Royalty Board (CRB): Judicial panel that sets rates for mechanical royalties and the digital public performance of sound recordings, https://www.crb.gov/.
Library of Congress (LOC): Official library of the legislative branch that houses the Copyright Office, https://www.loc.gov/.
U.S. Congress: Establishes America's copyright laws, https://www.congress.gov/.
U.S. Copyright Office (USCO): Official copyright registration and recordation body that advises Congress and the public on copyright matters and sets rules for copyright under statutory mandate, https://www.copyright.gov/.
U.S. Department of Justice (DOJ): Among other things, oversees ASCAP and BMI consent decrees, https://www.justice.gov/.
U.S. Patent and Trademark Organization (USPTO): Official registration and recordation body for patents and trademarks that engages on copyright matters in coordination with the USCO, https://www.uspto.gov/.
U.S. Trade Representative (USTR): Represents America's trade interests and negotiates international treaties (including intellectual property), https://ustr.gov/.

NOTES

CHAPTER 1

1. The U.S. Copyright Act considers a work to be fixed "when its embodiment in a copy or phonorecord, by or under the authority of the author, is sufficiently permanent or stable to permit it to be perceived, reproduced, or otherwise communicated for a period of more than transitory duration. A work consisting of sounds, images, or both, that are being transmitted, is 'fixed' . . . if a fixation of the work is being made simultaneously with its transmission." See 17 U.S. Code § 105—Subject matter of copyright: United States Government works.

2. The Copyright Act defines this as "when its embodiment in a copy or phonorecord, by or under the authority of the author, is sufficiently permanent or stable to permit it to be perceived, reproduced, or otherwise communicated for a period of more than transitory duration. A work consisting of sounds, images, or both, that are being transmitted, is 'fixed' . . . if a fixation of the work is being made simultaneously with its transmission." See 17 U.S. Code § 105—Subject matter of copyright: United States Government works.

CHAPTER 2

1. The Western philosopher John Locke (1632–1704) advanced the idea of rights as natural and inalienable; these natural rights included one's life, liberty, and property.

2. "Article 1, Section 8, Clause 8: Thomas Jefferson to Isaac McPherson," n.d., accessed February 19, 2021, https://press-pubs.uchicago.edu/founders/documents/a1_8_8s12.html.

CHAPTER 3

1. See chapters 4 and 8 for more information on the Music Modernization Act of 2018.
2. "Radio Facts and Figures: News Generation: Broadcast Media Relations," News Generation, Inc., January 22, 2020, https://www.newsgeneration.com/broadcast-resources/radio-facts-and-figures/.
3. Ibid.
4. Emily M. Reigart, "U.S. Commercial Radio Revenue Down in 2017," *Radio World*, April 5, 2018, https://www.radioworld.com/news-and-business/radio-revenue-down-in-2017.
5. Ed Christman, "U.S. Music Industry Hits Highest Revenue Mark in a Decade, Fueled by Paid Subscriptions," *Billboard*, March 26, 2018, accessed July 25, 2018, https://www.billboard.com/articles/business/8257558/us-music-industry-2017-highest-revenue-in-decade-fueled-paid-subscriptions.
6. *Sony Corp. of America v. Universal City Studios, Inc.*, 464 U.S. 417 (1984) cleared the way for home video and shields products from copyright liability if the product has substantial noninfringing uses.
7. That is, until 2009, when Jobs decided to get rid of DRM for music sold on iTunes. DRM lives on in the world of on-demand streaming, though most listeners don't notice as tracks play seamlessly across devices and music can be "shared" with other users.
8. Mark Sweney, "Music Industry Goes to War with YouTube," *The Guardian*, April 15, 2017, accessed July 30, 2018, https://www.theguardian.com/business/2017/apr/15/music-industry-youtube-video-streaming-royalties.

CHAPTER 4

1. "RIAA: The License Has Landed," *Wired*, October 9, 2001, accessed September 26, 2018, https://www.wired.com/2001/10/riaa-the-license-has-landed/.
2. As of this writing, the rates are 11.4 percent of revenue with a scheduled annual increase of around 1 percent annually through the new rate term, reaching 15.1 percent in 2022.

NOTES

3. Direct deals between publishers and services are also permitted under MMA.

4. "BMI Sets Revenue Records with $1.199 Billion," BMI.com, September 12, 2018, accessed February 6, 2019, https://www.bmi.com/news/entry/bmi-sets-revenue-records-with-1.199-billion.

5. In the United States, there is no public performance of downloads of audio tracks containing underlying compositions. However, interactive (or on-demand) streaming does constitute a public performance (though it is a much smaller percentage, around 6 to 7 percent of service gross revenue).

6. Improvised performances captured in a tangible medium or otherwise transmitted are eligible for copyright if the expression is original enough to warrant protection.

7. 17 U.S.C. §101.

8. No, it's not.

CHAPTER 5

1. Eric Alper, "It Costs at Least $500,000 to Break a New Artist," That Eric Alper, January 7, 2018, https://www.thatericalper.com/2014/11/30/it-costs-at-least-500000-to-break-a-new-artist/.

CHAPTER 6

1. "User Clip: Lars Ulrich before SJC," The Future of Digital Music, CSPAN, July 11, 2000. https://www.c-span.org/video/?c4740595%2Fuser-clip-lars-ulrich-sjc.

2. Frank Catalano, "From Rhapsody to Napster: How This Pioneering Music Service Coulda Been Spotify—and Why It Isn't," GeekWire, April 14, 2018, https://www.geekwire.com/2018/rhapsody-napster-pioneering-music-service-coulda-spotify-isnt/.

3. Glenn Sansone, "CMJ New Music Report," *College Music Journal*, May 8, 2000.

4. Eric Pfanner, "Music Industry Counts the Cost of Piracy," *New York Times*, January 21, 2010, https://www.nytimes.com/2010/01/22/business/global/22music.html.

5. David Kravets, "File Sharing Lawsuits at a Crossroads, After 5 Years of RIAA Litigation," *Wired*, n.d., accessed February 20, 2021, https://www.wired.com/2008/09/proving-file-sh/.

6. Eric Bangeman, "RIAA Trial Verdict Is In: Jury Finds Thomas Liable for Infringement," Ars Technica, October 4, 2007, https://arstechnica.com/tech-policy/2007/10/verdict-is-in/.

7. "*RIAA v. The People*: Five Years Later," Electronic Frontier Foundation, October 6, 2011, https://www.eff.org/wp/riaa-v-people-five-years-later.

8. Peter Lauria, "INFRINGEMENT!" *New York Post*, February 27, 2008, https://nypost.com/2008/02/27/infringement/.

9. Eric Bangeman, "RIAA Anti-P2P Campaign a Real Money Pit, According to Testimony," Ars Technica, October 3, 2007, https://arstechnica.com/tech-policy/2007/10/music-industry-exec-p2p-litigation-is-a-money-pit/.

10. "Record Labels Sue Megaupload For Massive Copyright Theft," RIAA, March 11, 2020, https://www.riaa.com/record-labels-sue-megaupload-for-massive-copyright-theft/.

11. Cyrys Farivar, "Kim Dotcom Settles Case He Filed against NZ Police over 'Military-Style Raid,'" Ars Technica, November 3, 2017, https://arstechnica.com/tech-policy/2017/11/kim-dotcom-settles-case-he-filed-against-nz-police-over-military-style-raid/.

12. "Article 1, Section 8, Clause 8: Thomas Jefferson to Isaac McPherson," accessed February 19, 2021, https://press-pubs.uchicago.edu/founders/documents/a1_8_8s12.html.

13. Gene Markin, "Internet Service Provider (ISP) Cox Communications Found Liable to the Tune of $1 Billion for Allowing Users to Illegally Share Music Files on Peer-to-Peer Networks," *The National Law Review*, November 12, 2020, https://www.natlawreview.com/article/internet-service-provider-isp-cox-communications-found-liable-to-tune-1-billion.

14. *Sony Corp. of America v. Universal City Studios, Inc.*, 464 U.S. 417 (1984).

15. Mike Masnick, "Breaking News: Feds Falsely Censor Popular Blog for Over a Year, Deny All Due Process, Hide All Details . . ." Techdirt, December 8, 2011, https://www.techdirt.com/articles/20111208/08225217010/breaking-news-feds-falsely-censor-popular-blog-over-year-deny-all-due-process-hide-all-details.shtml.

16. Brendan Sasso, "White House Weighs In on Internet Piracy Battle," *The Hill*, February 3, 2016, https://thehill.com/policy/technology/204171-white-house-weighs-in-on-internet-piracy-battle.

17. Lew Harris, "White House: Anti-Piracy Legislation Must Not Curtail Innovation, Freedom of Expression," *Reuters*, January 14, 2012, https://www.reuters.com/article/idUS245775808320120114.

18. Ibid.

19. Paul Resnikoff, "Zoe Keating: The Battle over Piracy Doesn't Really Include Artists," *Digital Music News*, July 21, 2020, https://www.digitalmusicnews.com/2012/01/24/keating/.

20. Chris Eggertsen, "How the Recording Academy and Its Industry Allies Scored Big Wins in the Pandemic Relief Bill," *Billboard*, January 15, 2021, https://www.billboard.com/articles/business/9511645/pandemic-relief-bill-music-industry-save-our-stages-case-act/.

21. 17 U.S. Code § 512—Limitations on liability relating to material online.

22. Ibid.

23. *Capitol Records, LLC v. Vimeo, LLC*, 972 F. Supp. 2d 500, 972 F. Supp. 2d 537 (S.D.N.Y. 2013).

24. Sam Byford, "Grooveshark Is Dead," The Verge, May 1, 2015, https://www.theverge.com/2015/4/30/8526105/grooveshark-shuts-down-settles-with-labels.

25. Ben Sisario, "YouTube Reaches Settlement over Songwriting Royalties," *New York Times*, December 8, 2016, https://www.nytimes.com/2016/12/08/business/media/youtube-reaches-settlement-over-songwriting-royalties.html?_r=0.

26. Nate Mook, "RIAA Sues Deceased Grandmother," BetaNews, February 4, 2005, https://betanews.com/2005/02/04/riaa-sues-deceased-grandmother/.

27. One way to do that would be to expand the definition of "technical measures" found in subsection (i) of Section 512 of the DMCA.

28. "Medium: Five Stubborn Truths about YouTube and The Value Gap," RIAA, September 15, 2017, https://www.riaa.com/medium-five-stubborn-truths-youtube-value-gap/.

29. Ibid.

30. David Souter, "*Campbell v. Acuff-Rose Music*, 510 U.S. 569 (1994)," Legal Information Institute, March 7, 1994, https://www.law.cornell.edu/supct/html/92-1292.ZO.html.

31. Jomatami, "Rick Beato Calls Out 'Ridiculous Practice of Blocking and Demonetizing Educational YouTube Videos,'" Ultimate Guitar, April 5, 2019, https://www.ultimate-guitar.com/news/general_music_news/rick_beato_calls_out_ridiculous_practice_of_blocking__demonetizing_educational_youtube_videos.html.

32. Dylan Gilbert, "The Online Censorship Machine Is Revving Up: Here Are a Few Lessons Learned," Public Knowledge, February 26, 2020, https://

www.publicknowledge.org/blog/the-online-censorship-machine-is-revving-up-here-are-a-few-lessons-learned/.

33. *James W. Newton, Jr., v. Michael Diamond*, 388 F.3d 1189 (9th Cir. 2003).

34. Another case, *VMG Salsoul v. Ciccone* 824 F.3d 871 (9th Cir. 2016), involves Madonna's sample of a recorded horn part from "Ooh I Love It (Love Break)" by Salsoul Orchestra. Though the decision does not implicate fair use, it does provide for *de minimis* use of sound recordings. "We find Bridgeport's reasoning unpersuasive," the Ninth Circuit opinion states. It remains to be seen whether the tension between lower courts will eventually result in the Supreme Court hearing a case along these lines.

35. "More Information on Fair Use," U.S. Copyright Office, accessed February 20, 2021, https://www.copyright.gov/fair-use/more-info.html.

36. *Lenz v. Universal Music Corp.*, 572 F. Supp. 2d 1150, 1152 (N.D. Cal. 2008) (citing Stephanie Lenz, "Let's Go Crazy #1," YouTube, February 7, 2007, https://www.youtube.com/watch?v=N1KfJHFWlhQ).

37. *Lenz*, 572 F. Supp. 2d at 1154 (citing 17 U.S.C. § 512(c)(3)(A)(v)).

38. Ibid. (quoting *Rossi v. Motion Picture Ass'n of Am.*, 391 F.3d 1000, 1004 (9th Cir. 2004)).

39. *Lenz v. Universal Music Corp.*, 801 F.3d 1126 (2015), (9th Cir. 2015).

CHAPTER 7

1. "Fixed in a Tangible Medium of Expression," Legal Information Institute, accessed February 20, 2021, https://www.law.cornell.edu/wex/fixed_in_a_tangible_medium_of_expression#:~:text=Under%20the%20Copyright%20Act%2C%20a,of%20more%20than%20transitory%20duration.

2. *Berne Convention for the Protection of Literary and Artistic Works*, September 9, 1886, art. 6bis, S. Treaty Doc. No. 27, 99th Cong., 2d Sess. 41 (1986).

3. "Copyright Office Circular #4," U.S. Copyright Office, accessed February 20, 2021, https://copyright.gov/circs/circ04.pdf.

4. "Copyright Office Circular #34," U.S. Copyright Office, accessed February 20, 2021, https://www.copyright.gov/circs/circ34.pdf.

5. Recall that attribution is part of "moral rights" that the United States does not recognize. There has been in recent years a push by songwriters and some publishers to get streaming interactive services to include songwriter and producer credits on their platforms, with incremental success.

6. Allen Bargfrede, "Shared Data Can Transform the Music Industry," Medium, June 22, 2020, https://medium.com/verifimedia/shared-data-can-transform-the-music-industry-162ff9d293c9.

7. Ibid.

8. Benji Rogers, "The DotBlockchain Music Project—Update #7 Minimum Viable Data Doc," Medium, September 23, 2019, https://medium.com/verifimedia/the-dotblockchain-music-project-update-7-minimum-viable-data-doc-561fdfadd5eb.

9. One such effort, the Global Repertoire Database, was a 2009 EU initiative that included key music stakeholders from all corners of the industry, including Apple, Amazon, Google, and music publishers. Talks broke down in 2014, with conflicts over governance, expenses, and concerns about redundancy among rights societies and PROs. In 2011, the former head of Geffen Records's technology division, Jim Griffin, partnered with the World Intellectual Property Organization to spearhead the International Music Registry, which succumbed to infighting between labels and publishers.

CHAPTER 8

1. BMI also entered a consent decree in 1941; ASCAP's was last amended in 2001, and BMI's in 1994.

2. Halle Kiefer, "Final Plea: Stop Soundtracking Movie Trailers with Somber, On-the-Nose Covers," *Vulture*, March 8, 2017, https://www.vulture.com/2017/03/movie-trailer-song-covers-please-stop.html.

3. Future of Music Coalition has the most detailed guide to copyright termination I've come across: https://cutt.ly/xlmWslB.

CHAPTER 9

1. Stuart Dredge, "US Recorded Music Revenues Grew 9.2% in 2020 Despite Covid-19," Music Ally, March 1, 2021, https://musically.com/2021/03/01/us-recorded-music-revenues-grew-9-2-in-2020-despite-covid-19/.

2. Tim Ingham, "New Music Drops Every Minute. But Back-Catalogs Are Driving the Industry's Transformation," *Rolling Stone*, September 8, 2020, https://www.rollingstone.com/pro/features/music-catalogs-value-keeps-rising-could-it-change-the-face-of-the-entire-industry-1056229/.

INDEX

aggregators, 59, 103, 106, 129, 140; Distrokid, 59, 106, 129; CD Baby, 46, 59, 77, 106, 129; Tunecore, 46, 59, 77, 106, 129
AM/FM radio, 10, 26, 27, 42, 47, 58, 62–64, 116, 124
Amazon Music, 32, 44, 140, 155
American Association of Independent Music (A2IM), 72, 75, 145
American Federation of Musicians (AFM), 63, 145
Apple Music, 26, 31–32, 42, 44, 70, 132, 136, 140

Blockchain, 90, 103, 108–11; minimum viable data, 105–6, 109

compulsory license, 9–10, 39, 41, 45, 49, 58, 103, 114, 130
Content ID, 79–80
Copyright, xi-xvi; sound recording copyright, xi, xv, 4–5, 7–11, 21, 25, 27, 29, 35, 37, 43, 51, 57–65, 83, 84, 96–99, 101–5, 113–15, 124–38; musical works copyright, xv, 5–7, 9, 20–21, 27, 35, 37–53, 101–15
copyright exclusive rights, 2, 8, 21, 37–38, 55, 57–58, 64–65, 86, 95; Reproduction/distribution rights, 3, 9, 19–20, 25, 38–40, 43, 48, 57, 58, 101, 129; Adaptations/derivative works rights, 10, 38, 48–51, 54, 58, 64, 99; public display rights, 11, 38, 51; public performance rights, 7, 10, 20, 28, 46–48, 52, 57–61, 65, 114–17, 125
copyright legislation: 1790 Copyright Act, 14, 20; 1976 Copyright Act, 7–8, 23, 48, 137; Copyright Alternative in Small Claims Enforcement Act of 2019 (CASE Act), 75; Section 115 of Copyright Act of 1976, 40–41, 44; Digital Performance

Right in Sound Recordings Act of 1995 (DPRA), 114, 124; Digital Millenium Copyright Act of 1998 (DMCA), 33–34, 75–80, 85–86; Stop Online Piracy Act (SOPA), 71–75; Music Modernization Act of 2018 (MMA), 40–47, 55, 117–18, 126
Copyright Office, 8, 37, 41, 45, 54, 75, 84, 89–101
copyright registration, 93–100
Copyright Royalty Board, 40, 63, 124
copyright termination, 8, 137, 138
copyright terms, 4, 19

de minimis use, 83, 84

fair use, 10, 50, 64, 67, 81, 83–86

infringement, 3, 9, 32–33, 37, 41, 67, 69–78, 80–82, 86–87, 90, 92, 94, 99
International Standard Recording Code (ISRC), 102, 105–7

joint works, 53–55, 94

Kobalt, 53, 129

Library of Congress, 91, 111

master recordings/masters, 7, 125
master use license, 61, 64, 113–14, 132–33, 137–38

synchronization, 38, 46, 52, 53, 58, 61, 64, 113, 114, 124, 129–33, 138

metadata, 7, 79, 80, 89, 95, 101–4, 106–8, 122, 126

Napster, 13, 32, 67–69, 104
National Music Publishers Association (NMPA), 42, 45, 73, 78

peer-to-peer file-sharing (P2P), 32–33, 67–68, 77, 86
performing rights organizations (PROs) and mechanical royalty collectives, 20–21, 46–48, 52, 103–4, 113–23; American Society of Composers, Authors and Publishers (ASCAP), 21, 28, 46–47, 52, 114–23, 146; Broadcast Music, Inc. (BMI), 28, 46–47, 52, 114–23; Global Music Rights (GMR), 47, 52, 115, 117–19; Harry Fox Agency, 43, 117, 127; Mechanical Licensing Collective (MLC), 41, 45–46, 53, 126–28; SESAC, 43, 46–47, 52, 115, 117–19, 127
piracy, 3, 29, 67–68, 71, 75, 142
podcasts, 102, 136
public domain, 4–5, 14, 19, 29, 39, 48–50

Recording Industry Association of America (RIAA), 42, 69–74, 80, 139
Register of Copyrights, 45, 91
royalties:
 royalty rate, 39, 41, 63;
 Mechanical royalties, 25–26, 30, 39–47, 52–53, 63, 124, 126, 128–29; performance royalties, 26–28, 46, 52, 58, 114, 121, 123, 129, 135

safe harbors, 33–34, 67, 76–81
Sirius XM, 125, 136

SoundExchange, 58, 63, 113, 123–28
Spotify, 26, 32–34, 42–44, 71, 80, 100, 102, 125, 127, 136, 140

transparency, 35, 45, 89, 101, 109

YouTube, 33–34, 46, 59, 77–81, 85

ABOUT THE AUTHOR

Casey Rae is an author, professor, musician, and music business professional based in Vancouver, Washington. As director of music licensing for SiriusXM, he oversees the licensing of audio for transmission across the company's services. Previously, Casey served as the CEO of the Future of Music Coalition, a Washington, DC–based education and advocacy organization for musicians and composers. He has authored and teaches courses at Georgetown University and Berklee College of Music on copyright, digital disruption, and media policy. Casey regularly speaks on issues such as emerging business models, creators' rights, technology policy, and intellectual property at worldwide conferences, universities, and in the media. He has testified before the U.S. Congress on copyright matters and has written hundreds of articles on the impact of technology on the music community in scholarly journals and other publications. His book *William S. Burroughs and the Cult of Rock 'n' Roll*, an exploration of the Beat writer's impact on music culture, has been translated into four languages across six editions. Casey serves on the board of the Alliance for Media Arts and Culture and the MHz Foundation and is the proud dad of two talented daughters.

www.ingramcontent.com/pod-product-compliance
Lightning Source LLC
Chambersburg PA
CBHW061838300426
44115CB00013B/2434